The Conversation on Higher Ed

Critical Conversations

Martin LaMonica, Series Editor

The Conversation U.S. is an independent, nonprofit news organization dedicated to delivering expert knowledge to the public through journalism. Every day The Conversation produces 10–12 stories through a collaboration between scholars and editors, with the scholars writing explanatory journalism and analysis based on their research and the editors helping them translate it into plain language. The articles can be read on TheConversation.com and have been republished by more than a thousand newspapers and websites through a Creative Commons license, meaning that the content is always free to read and republish.

The book series Critical Conversations is published collaboratively by The Conversation U.S. and Johns Hopkins University Press. Each volume in the series features a curated selection of subject-specific articles from The Conversation and is guest-edited by an expert scholar of the subject.

■

The Conversation on Higher Ed is guest-edited by Mary L. Churchill, Professor of the Practice and Associate Dean of Strategic Partnerships and Community Engagement at Boston University's Wheelock College of Education and Human Development.

Martin LaMonica is the Series Editor, Critical Conversations.
Chris Calimlim is the Editorial Assistant.
Beth Daley is the Executive Editor and General Manager of The Conversation U.S.
Bruce Wilson is the Chief Innovation and Development Officer of The Conversation U.S.

We would like to express our gratitude to the editors and scholars who produced the articles collected here and to thank our colleagues and funders who allow us to do this important work in the public interest.

THE CONVERSATION
on Higher Ed

edited by Mary L. Churchill

Johns Hopkins University Press

BALTIMORE

© 2025 Johns Hopkins University Press
All rights reserved. Published 2025
Printed in the United States of America on acid-free paper
9 8 7 6 5 4 3 2 1

Johns Hopkins University Press
2715 North Charles Street
Baltimore, Maryland 21218
www.press.jhu.edu

Library of Congress Cataloging-in-Publication Data is available.

A catalog record for this book is available from the British Library.

ISBN 978-1-4214-5139-8 (paperback)
ISBN 978-1-4214-5140-4 (ebook)

*Special discounts are available for bulk purchases of this book. For more
information, please contact Special Sales at specialsales@jh.edu.*

Contents

Part II.
Why College Still Matters   49

Part III.
Education as a Private Good   81

Part IV.
Inequality and the Failure of Social Systems   109

Higher Education under the Microscope

HIGHER EDUCATION HAS BEEN IN THE NEWS often in recent years—and not always in a good way. There's been a flood of headlines on the burden of student loan debt; the mental health challenges of students; attacks on diversity, race, and inclusion programs; and many other flash points in our country's culture wars.

One news story stands out in my memory because it seemed to cast doubt on the value of higher education itself. Published in 2021 mid-pandemic in the *Wall Street Journal*, the story's headline said it all: "A Generation of American Men Give Up on College: 'I Just Feel Lost.'"

I had a son in college at the time, so the trend reported in the article hit close to home. But it also felt like a generational change. When I graduated from high school, I was intimidated by the cost of going to college, yet I never questioned whether it would be worth it. Indeed, the notion that higher education is crucial to one's future prospects was baked into my personal narrative: my father was the first in his family to go to college, opening up professional opportunities that his older siblings couldn't even consider.

The value of higher education is just one of the important themes this book addresses head-on. It's designed to give students and parents an understanding of what it takes to succeed in college today—and it takes up higher education's role in society overall as well. In addition to containing practical articles on applying to and paying for college, it covers broader issues many students will face in college, including inequality, diversity, student activism, artificial intelligence, and online learning as well as academic freedom and free speech.

Guest-edited by education policy expert Mary L. Churchill of Boston University, this volume collects articles that were previously published in The Conversation, a news analysis and explanatory journalism website, and written by academics and edited by journalists. Our stories are grounded in the latest academic research but are aimed at a general audience, rather than other experts. In putting together this collection, we have lightly edited the contributions to remove dated references or, in some cases, to update statistics.

College campuses have long been at the forefront of social debates as places to advance new ideas. But the accelerated pace of change in recent years has led more people to consider alternatives to a traditional four-year degree. Amid all the tumult, this book, written by people with deep knowledge of the subjects covered, answers many of the pressing questions that incoming students and their families face. It also helps us all see where higher education is headed in the future.

Martin LaMonica

Preface

WE ARE AT A MAJOR INFLECTION POINT within higher education and society. Even as the higher education sector is under siege, there has never been a more crucial time for the important work we are doing on our campuses, be they brick and mortar or online. Higher education will be critical to overcoming the current challenges facing our democracy and our workforce. But while our elite institutions provide some of the world's best training for the global elite, we are failing to bring that same level of care and concern to educating the non-elite young people who may live across the street from our universities and colleges.

At a time in our country's history when we have made great gains for women students, students of color, and first-generation students, we are being told that "not everyone needs to go to college." When we were just getting to a point where most young people growing up in this country thought they would go to college, we seem to have hit our peak and be in decline. For our country and its people to thrive, we need to reverse this emerging pattern and do so quickly. I remain an eternal optimist with great hope for a better future. I believe that we have phenomenal opportunities for turning the current situation around. Below, I outline the current state of higher education and point to fixes for its problems—in order to fix our country.

Current State of Education in the United States

By now, it is familiar news that higher education is heading to the edge of an enrollment cliff. Beginning with the 2025–26 academic year, colleges will start to feel the impact of a drop in birth rates over the last 15–20 years—what demographer Nathan Grawe refers to as the "evolving birth dearth."[1] Between 2025 and 2029, we will see a 15% decline in the number of 18-year-olds graduating from high school in the United States.

Declining birth rates aren't the only challenge hitting society and higher education, however. We are also facing a demand cliff.[2] In 2016, 70% of recent high school graduates were enrolled in college; in 2021 and 2022, that rate was 62%. So, not only are there fewer 18-year-olds who could go to college because of lower birth rates; there are also fewer high school students who are interested in attending college. The "birth dearth" means that maintaining college enrollments at their current rates would require that more students go to college right out of high school so that college enrollment rates for all would increase by 12%. It took the United States

10 years to get from 60% to 70% college attendance (2006 to 2016), and now those rates are falling.[3]

This drop has been sharpest for male students and white students. The proportion of male students who go straight from high school to college was 63% in 2010 and had decreased to 55% by 2021; for white students, this rate of enrollment following high school dropped over the same period from 70% to 64%. The overall college enrollment rate for 18- to 24-year-olds in the United States has also decreased, from 41% in 2010 to 38% in 2021. Between fall 2010 and fall 2021, total undergraduate enrollment in degree-granting postsecondary institutions in the United States decreased by 15% (from 18.1 million to 15.4 million students).[4]

Across the globe, public education is the major societal structure that turns a country's people from residents into engaged citizens. Here in the United States, two of the most important things that education has historically done for society are instilling a sense of pride and responsibility for our country's democratic experiment and preparing young people for an increasingly complex workforce. Heather McGhee and Victor Ray articulated these purposes in a recent *New York Times* op-ed: "we have public schools to make young people into educated, productive adults. But public schools are also for making Americans. Thus, public education requires lessons about history—the American spirit and its civics—and also contact with and context about other Americans: who we are and what has made us."[5] Unfortunately, the enrollment cliff is meeting a demand cliff at a time when democracy in our country is under threat, when the need for a more highly skilled workforce in a knowledge economy is growing, and when a robust and fully enrolled prekindergarten-to-bachelors-degree education system (commonly referred to as PK–16) is needed more than ever before.

Considering education trends in the United States within a global context can be quite illuminating, especially when thinking through how these trends might play out in the near future. The United Nations has the Human Development Index (HDI), a useful tool for comparing education levels and trends across countries. The HDI combines measures of a population's life expectancy, education levels, and per capita income for a country. There are currently 69 countries in the HDI's "very high human development" tier; as of 2022, the United States was ranked twentieth, having dropped five spots in a single year, down from fifteenth in 2021.[6] We could blame COVID for this drop, but COVID was a pandemic with global impact, and our education levels had already begun to drop before COVID.

While countries like the Republic of Korea and Slovenia are making rapid gains across education levels, attainment of education benchmarks in the United States has started to slow down and, in some instances, taper off. While the United States has relatively strong rates of high school graduation (fifth in world rankings, after the Republic of Korea, Slovenia, Canada, and Ireland), the rate of increase is slowing. When it comes to college degree attainment, the United States continues to make gains, as do all but 1 of 38 countries belonging to the Organisation for Economic Co-operation and Development (OECD). However, as of 2022, the Republic of Korea is in first place, with 69% of its younger citizens having attained a college degree, while the United States is ranked twelfth. For bachelor's degree attainment, the Republic of Korea is at the top with 45%, and the United

States is at 29%. For master's degree attainment, Luxembourg is in first place with 38%, and the United States, at 11%, is lower than the OECD country average of 15%. In other words, other countries are significantly outpacing us.[7]

The state of higher education in the United States looks a little rosier when we consider college rankings alone. In *Times Higher Education*'s 2024 rankings of colleges and universities around the world, seven of the top institutions are in the United States. These elite institutions serve only a fraction of our resident college-going population, however. The international student body at those seven US institutions ranges from 21% at Yale to 33% at the Massachusetts Institute of Technology and the California Institute of Technology.[8] The bottom line is that we are not educating our resident population as well as we could be or as well as many other countries are—and we are educating fewer and fewer of them.

Education as a Public Good

Education is a necessary component of a well-functioning democracy, especially in an increasingly knowledge-based economy. Historically, there has been a strong relationship between democracy and education. Democracy is more than a political system; ideally, it is also a way of life, in which we treat one another equitably and understand the need to balance individual rights with commitments and responsibilities toward others. In *Longing for Justice: Higher Education and Democracy's Agenda*, Jennifer S. Simpson frames democracy as a "form of sociality," that is, "a way to be human" and to "live together well."[9] Democracy, when framed this way, is an aspiration that is necessarily ongoing and unfinished. At their best, our colleges and universities, like our public primary and secondary schools, have an important role to play in strengthening our country's democracy, which many of us believe is under threat. Simpson refers to this role as the "social contract higher education has with public life."[10]

Along with threats to our democracy, our country's current and future workforce is in danger of being underprepared. In 2021, about 68% of all jobs in the United States required at least some postsecondary education. Researchers at the Center on Education and the Workforce at Georgetown University predict that, by 2031, 72% of US jobs will require postsecondary education or training and that 42% will require at least a bachelor's degree. Only 28% of jobs will go to workers with a high school diploma or less, a drop from 32% for graduating seniors in 2024. Between 2021 and 2031, there will be 18.5 million job openings per year on average, some 12.5 million of which will require at least some college education.[11]

These projections present a stark view of the importance of college education in preparing the future workforce. The US economy is now divided between a large but stagnant blue-collar economy and a smaller but faster-growing professional economy. This is leading to a widening economic divide between those who have postsecondary education and those who do not. Postsecondary education is no longer just the preferred pathway to middle-class jobs and a family-sustaining wage; it is, increasingly, the only pathway. Of course, there will always be exceptions—look at Mark Zuckerberg and Bill Gates. We in the United States love to doubt trends in data by pointing to maverick outliers, yet the data tell a powerful story.

Research shows us again and again that, on average, college graduates are wealthier and healthier. They are more likely to have stable marriages and be involved in their communities, and they are less likely to be in trouble with the criminal justice system. The higher income that results from a college degree is sometimes referred to as the "college wage premium," and it has grown with time. Over the course of a lifetime, the average college graduate with a bachelor's degree will earn twice as much as the average person without a degree, in good part because jobs that require a college education are usually better paying (and take place in safer work environments). Workers with more education also tend to have a lower average rate of unemployment.[12]

So Why Aren't Students Going to College?

And yet, many of our young people don't want to go to college.

A recent Gallup and Carnegie Foundation poll found that 39% of parents who had hoped their child would enroll in college or a training program after high school reported that their child did not.[13] The media tells us that not everyone needs to go to college but also that we need a college-educated workforce now more than ever. Jamie Merisotis at the Lumina Foundation highlights the key reasons we need even more people with college credentials, not fewer. Two of those stand out: First, people need college so they can earn a family-sustaining wage. Within the next 10 years, more than two-thirds of jobs that offer good pay and benefits will require at least some college. Second, we need an educated workforce to fill these positions.[14] According to the US

Chamber of Commerce, there are 8.8 million job openings in the United States and 6.4 million unemployed workers. Even if every unemployed person in the country was working, there would still be close to 2.4 million open jobs.[15] In the last two years, in recovering from the pandemic-driven downturn in the economy, we have experienced the highest inflation in 40 years and the lowest rate of unemployment in 50 years. Current employment rates are highest among 25- to 34-year-olds with bachelor's degrees or more and lowest for those without a high school diploma.[16]

So why are we seeing less demand for college? We all know that college has become more expensive, but the real cost of college has also become more difficult to determine. Some of the most expensive private institutions now offer to cover full tuition plus fees for lower-income students and families, and tuition discount rates at non-elite institutions continue to rise. This is confusing and mysterious to those of us who work in higher education and impossible to understand for many college students, especially first-generation students and their families. Not surprisingly, we now have what Grawe calls the "perception of financial inaccessibility" for college among low-income students.[17] He finds that Black and Hispanic students are especially prone to overestimating the price of tuition, when private institutions are most financially inaccessible to middle-income families. In other words, the confusion, perceptions, and realities of the cost of a college education have themselves become a barrier.

With the unemployment rate at a historic low and entry-level jobs aplenty, a team I advised at one public college in New Jersey said that "Amazon is our biggest competitor." Post-pandemic, wages have increased, especially for entry-level positions, and giving up a weekly paycheck and paying for college is a double financial hit that many young people are unable or unwilling to take. Instead, they are pocketing short-term money today in favor of the long-term financial stability and family-sustaining income more likely for those with a college education.[18]

Despite these obstacles, I believe that the world, and especially our country, needs higher education now more than ever. We need higher education because of the knowledge economy, because of threats to democracy, because of the increasingly difficult challenges we are facing environmentally, and because of growing inequality. A more educated society could help us address all these issues, but instead we are moving in the wrong direction. How do we reverse this decline and rise to meet these educational and global crises?

Partnering with School Districts

The first step is to integrate education across the lifespan, to think holistically about education for society, and in so doing to build the pipeline to college. We do this by embedding higher education with primary and secondary education through partnerships with local districts. While we can't magically create more high school graduates, we can work to change the downward trajectory of the demand cliff. Deep partnerships between colleges and universities and their local school districts create pathways to college that show our young people and their families that a college education can be attainable and affordable.

A college-going identity starts to set in during middle school. In my work with Harvard's Project on Workforce and Boston University's Center for Future Readiness, I've learned quite a bit about the importance of transition work related to college and career pathways. One important tool in this work is MyCAP, which stands for My Career and Academic Plan. MyCAP is a student-driven multiyear preparation that has been implemented in many school districts in Massachusetts and other states. It guides students in creating a postsecondary plan for success after high school. Research shows that the use of MyCAP improves student engagement, attendance, and understanding of the connection between education and future aspirations. Beginning as early as sixth grade, students engage in activities that help them answer big questions: *Who am I?* and *What do I want to do?* and *How do I get there?* These questions align with three domains of college and career readiness: personal and social, career development, and academic planning. Beginning in seventh grade, students start to make connections between academic success in middle school, future success in high school and college, and career goals. MyCAP reaches young people before they have decided that college isn't for them and shows them that they can go to college.[19]

Another partnership is dual enrollment. In dual-enrollment programs, college professors teach college-credit-bearing courses to high school students. These are often exploratory courses, such as a survey of health care, or college preparatory courses, such as college writing or college algebra. Dual-enrollment programs have grown tremendously in recent years. Today, 88% of high schools offer their students opportunities to earn college credits, and increasing numbers of schools are including dual enrollment as an option along with Advanced Placement courses.[20]

What is called *early college* is a form of dual enrollment that offers a cohort-based experience and builds in student supports. Early college is a partnership between school districts or high schools and two- or four-year colleges or universities. It offers students the opportunity to earn an associate's degree or up to two years of college credits toward a bachelor's degree while attending high school—at no or low cost. Early college also provides support to students as they plan for their college education, including helping them select college courses, transfer to four-year colleges, and identify sources of financial aid.

Direct admission is another way that colleges are bridging the divide between secondary and postsecondary education. Direct admission can be done at the state or university level. At the institutional level, a college or university partners with a local high school to offer admission to those high schoolers who meet the minimum requirements for entry after graduation, which typically call for a certain grade point average (GPA), set of courses, standardized test score, or a combination thereof. At the state level, a state's department of education or higher education organizes an acceptance letter that is sent out to high school seniors, offering them admission to an institution from a list of public colleges and universities in the state. Depending on the program's standards of eligibility, some institutions might require a minimum GPA to qualify for direct admission. In California, for instance, California State University at Fresno is piloting a program to start direct admission as early as ninth grade. For students who do not think they can get into college or do not consider themselves to be college material, this offer can be life changing.[21]

The Common Application, or Common App, is a single online application that students use to apply to multiple institutions. Over 1,000 institutions now use it. Common App has been piloting a new direct admissions approach since 2021. On the basis of information that students provide, colleges coordinate with Common App to email potential applicants to let them know they will be accepted as soon as they submit an application. The 2022–23 pilot offered admission to nearly 30,000 students at 14 participating colleges. Results showed the impacts were strongest for Black, Latinx, and first-generation students.[22]

Colleges are also eliminating the requirement for standardized test scores so as to remove another enrollment barrier for populations who have historically been denied access to higher education.[23] Many institutions have gone test optional, and some have even gone test blind. Test-optional schools give applicants the option to submit SAT or ACT scores but do not require them to do so, while test-blind schools do not consider standardized test scores. Prior to the COVID-19 pandemic, in 2019, there were approximately 1,050 test-optional schools out of approximately 2,300 bachelor-degree-granting institutions, not counting four-year for-profit schools. In 2024, there are over 1,900 test-optional or test-blind schools (test-optional is still the norm). For many of the schools that went test optional, applications went up and applicant diversity increased.

Making College More Affordable

There are also moves across the country to make college more affordable. One approach is to make the first year or two of college tuition-free. This is happening mainly at community colleges but also at some public universities and a handful of private institutions. Over 60% of US states now offer a version of tuition-free community college, with funding coming from state and local sources. As Michelle Miller-Adams reminds us, high school was not always universal or publicly funded, and the movement to make at least some part of college tuition-free builds on the same arguments that were made over 100 years ago for universal publicly funded high school.[24] Educating people is good for society. If the standard a century ago was a high school diploma, the time to increase that standard to college is long overdue.

In addition to helping young people see that college is indeed for them, dual enrollment can also cut down on their college expenses. Some districts aim to deliver two years of college credit while students are still in high school so that they will graduate with a high school diploma and an associate's degree and have only two more years of college to pay for. Some colleges are rolling this out by adding an additional year of high school through "year 13" programs. In Massachusetts, the Early College Promise (ECP) pilot program builds on standard high school offerings for early college and gives students more time to earn an associate's degree or 60 transferable credits toward a bachelor's degree at no cost—within the familiar context of high school with its strong student supports. ECP is intentionally designed to empower students traditionally underserved by higher education; it is being piloted in districts where the majority of students are economically disadvantaged and focuses on Black and Latinx students, especially those whose college prospects were affected by the COVID-19 pandemic.[25]

The number of states offering tuition-free associate's degrees at community colleges also continues to rise. Many of these tuition-free community college initiatives are Promise Programs: a diverse set of programs that offer tuition-free college for recent high school graduates at specified colleges in a geographic area (city, county, or state). The first of these programs was the Kalamazoo Promise in Kalamazoo, Michigan, which launched in 2007. More and more governors are realizing the need for a more educated workforce as their state experiences the challenges of hiring a well-trained workforce in an increasingly knowledge-based economy. Promise Programs directly address that challenge.[26]

According to the Community College Research Center, community colleges enrolled around 41% of all undergraduate students in the United States in the 2020–21 academic year, which means that two of every five undergraduates were attending a community college.[27] In the fall of 2022, Jill Barshay noted that 20% of community college enrollments were high school students taking courses through dual-enrollment programs, which means that a significant portion of fall 2022 college enrollments were actually high school students dually enrolled in college courses. In other words, these programs that target high school students and community colleges are already making a difference in college enrollment. They have the potential to make a much greater difference as more schools, colleges and universities, communities, and states embark upon them.[28]

Retention Strategies

Along with increasing the number of young people who enroll in college, we need to focus our efforts on keeping students enrolled once they show up in college classes—whether on campus, online, or at their high schools. Fortunately, great efforts have been made in increasing the retention and successful progression of students toward degree completion.

In *Paying the Price*, Sara Goldrick-Rab reframes the true cost of college by emphasizing that one of the biggest reasons why students stop going to classes is that they can't afford basic living expenses.[29] Universities have realized that even when they provide full scholarships for tuition and make college tuition-free, poor and working-class students still can't afford to go to college. Why? Because they can't afford rent, food, transportation, health care, and digital access; these are referred to as basic needs. Colleges have responded by opening food pantries and helping students apply for benefits from a supplemental nutrition assistance program. Staff at food pantries on campuses also help students apply for subsidized housing and health care.

These campus initiatives are often a component of broader student success strategies. As colleges and universities recruit more diverse students, they need more diverse structures to support their success: for veteran students, student parents, part-time students, and students with disabilities, to name just a few types of students enrolled in our colleges and universities. Student support can't be one size fits all—and it never has been. We are now more aware, though, of how our policies and processes support the success (or not) of different groups on campus. We have learned to disaggregate our data to see what's working or not working and to identify for whom it is working and for whom it is not. For many of us, this is part of the equity-audit work we are doing on campus.

For the last few years, I have served as an advisor in the Learner Success Lab of the American Council on Education, where I've advised teams at public institutions in Oregon, New Jersey, and Ohio. Part of the lab's mission is to help colleges and universities retain and graduate the students they recruit. We look at courses, departments, and faculty with high DFW rates (grades of D, F, or withdraw) and look for the patterns behind these rates to see what's going on. Often it is something as simple as a strict late-to-class policy that runs up against public transportation delays. We also look for things like opportunities to provide supplemental instruction to students, typically through peer instructors, and the success rates of hybrid courses. The goal is to meet students where they are rather than waiting for them to come to us.

High-impact student engagement practices are another critical set of retention strategies. Many of these include work-based learning for college credit, such as co-ops, internships, and service learning. One of the most successful retention strategies for undergraduate students is an on-campus job. Dollar for dollar, it is one of the best investments in retention that we can make. On-campus jobs can replace off-campus jobs, which are generally less flexible and forgiving about class schedules, semester breaks, and final-exam weeks. On-campus jobs also provide additional space for students to build relationships with the college community, which in turn increases their engagement and helps them stay in school.

Moving beyond Traditional Students

While convincing high school students that college is for them and supporting them to stay in college once they get there are crucial to increasing enrollment, another solution is to develop new pathways to attract students after high school graduation. In addition to working with local high schools, two- and four-year colleges are working to strengthen transfer pathways. Many institutions are holding regular transfer summits that bring together faculty from community colleges and four-year colleges to align their course catalogs and curriculum maps to better advise students. Universities and colleges are also creating combined undergraduate and graduate programs, often referred to as 4+1 and 3+2 degrees, to create more seamless pathways from undergraduate study through graduate school.

Institutions are also expanding their recruitment efforts beyond traditional-aged students. They are creating pathways for paraprofessionals that that will help them move into professional roles, and they are actively recruiting adult learners and career changers. At a regional accreditation annual meeting, Michelle Weise, author of *Long Life Learning: Preparing for Jobs That Don't Even Exist Yet*,[30] told attendees, me included, that the first generation who will live to be 150 years old has already been born. She then asked all of the higher education professionals in the room what were we planning to do with folks from ages 30 to 150. We were speechless.

It is also crucial that we actively partner with employers. Increasingly, companies are offering their own educational pathways. Unemployment rates are so low that companies can't wait for students to graduate from college; instead, they are recruiting students right out of high school and doing their own in-house training. Some are even creating their own company colleges that focus solely on their immediate workforce needs. I worry that these business-first approaches will train our young people only for present needs, with their training becoming obsolete after a few years. Postsecondary education needs to carry college credit and needs to help us build a better tomorrow, not just a better worker today.

At a time when we need more education more than ever before, we are walking away from education. At a time when education can be more affordable than ever before, young people and their families, especially working-class and poor young people, are saying college is not for them. At a time when most states offer some form of free college, students are saying it's too expensive. At a time when the media is dominated by stories of impossible admissions standards, astronomical sticker prices for enrollment, massive student loan debt after graduation, and underemployed baristas with a useless college degree, the most expensive part of attending college for the average working-class kid is actually the cost of basic needs like housing, medical care, food, clothing, transportation, and digital access.

The fact that financial aid is built around full-time attendance, when most of our undergraduate students attend part-time, is a clear signal of who matters. But what if we changed that? What would it look like if we centered the majority, centered equity, and put the most disadvantaged at the center of our policy making?

If we don't do this, equity gaps in our country will continue to grow, and democracy will continue to be under threat, here and around the world. We will have a less healthy population that will be more expensive to care for. We will know less about how to care for our planet and one another. To avoid this version of our future, the world needs those of us who care about the future of higher education to find ways to be more flexible, to think more creatively, to envision a future student that may be very different from current students.

If COVID taught us one thing, it is that we are all connected. The work we do today for our future students will directly impact the society we will have tomorrow. As Simpson reminds us, "Democracy begins with the labour of hope, with a belief in what is possible."[31] This is not an *impossible* situation. We just need to begin with the belief that everyone deserves a college education, and we need to have the will to make it happen.

Notes

1. Nathan Grawe, *The Agile College: How Institutions Successfully Navigate Demographic Changes* (Baltimore: Johns Hopkins University Press, 2021), 13.
2. Rebecca Mathews, Bijan Warner, and Peter Stokes, "Managing the Demand Cliff," op-ed, *Inside Higher Ed*, October 16, 2023. https://www.insidehighered.com/opinion/views/2023/10/16/managing-other-enrollment-cliff-opinion.
3. National Center for Education Statistics, "Undergraduate Enrollment. Condition of Education," US Department of Education, Institute of Education Sciences, 2023. https://nces.ed.gov/programs/coe/indicator/cha.
4. National Center for Education Statistics, "Undergraduate Enrollment."
5. Heather C. McGhee and Victor Ray, "School Is for Making Citizens," *New York Times*, September 1, 2022. https://www.nytimes.com/2022/09/01/opinion/us-school-citizenship.html.
6. *Breaking the Gridlock: Reimagining Cooperation in a Polarized World* (New York: United Nations Development Programme, 2024). https://hdr.undp.org/content/human-development-report-2023-24.
7. Organisation for Economic Co-operation and Development, *Education at a Glance 2023: OECD Indicators* (Paris: OECD Publishing, 2023). https://doi.org/10.1787/e13bef63-en.

8. "World University Rankings 2024," *Times Higher Education*. https://www.timeshighereducation.com/world-university-rankings/2024/world-ranking.

9. Jennifer S. Simpson, *Longing for Justice: Higher Education and Democracy's Agenda* (Toronto: University of Toronto Press, 2014), 29–30.

10. Simpson, *Longing for Justice*, 40.

11. Anthony P. Carnevale, Nicole Smith, Martin Van Der Werf, and Michael C. Quinn, *After Everything: Projections of Jobs, Education, and Training Requirements through 2031* (Washington, DC: Georgetown University Center on Education and the Workforce, 2023). cew.georgetown.edu/Projections2031.

12. "Healthy People 2030," US Department of Health and Human Services, Office of Disease Prevention and Health Promotion. https://health.gov/healthypeople.

13. *Family Voices: Building Pathways from Learning to Meaningful Work*, Gallup and Carnegie Corporation of New York, 2021. https://www.carnegie.org/publications/family-voices-building-pathways-learning-meaningful-work/.

14. Jamie Merisotis, "Thinking about College? Don't Let COVID Fatigue Hold You Back," Lumina Foundation, March 25, 2024. https://www.luminafoundation.org/news-and-views/thinking-about-college-dont-let-covid-fatigue-hold-you-back/.

15. Stephanie Ferguson, "Understanding America's Labor Shortage," US Chamber of Commerce, May 2, 2024. https://www.uschamber.com/workforce/understanding-americas-labor-shortage.

16. Stephanie Ferguson, Jenna Shrove, and Isabella Lucy, "Data Deep Dive: The Workforce of the Future," US Chamber of Commerce, October 4, 2023. https://www.uschamber.com/workforce/data-deep-dive-the-workforce-of-the-future.

17. Grawe, *Agile College*, 96

18. Elissa Nadworny, "More than 1 Million Fewer Students Are in College. Here's How That Impacts the Economy," National Public Radio, January 13, 2022. https://www.npr.org/2022/01/13/1072529477/more-than-1-million-fewer-students-are-in-college-the-lowest-enrollment-numbers-.

19. "My Career and Academic Plan (MyCAP)," Massachusetts Department of Elementary and Secondary Education, accessed May 3, 2024. https://www.doe.mass.edu/ccte/sec-design/mycap/default.html.

20. Luke Rhine, "The Power of Dual Enrollment: The Equitable Expansion of College Access and Success," US Department of Education blog, September 1, 2022. https://blog.ed.gov/2022/09/the-power-of-dual-enrollment-the-equitable-expansion-of-college-access-and-success/.

21. Liam Knox, "A (Very) Early Admission Guarantee," *Inside Higher Ed*, January 22, 2024. https://www.insidehighered.com/news/admissions

/traditional-age/2024/01/22/fresno-state-guarantees-admission
-ninth-graders.

22. "How Common App Direct Admissions Works," CommonApp.org, accessed May 5, 2024. https://www.commonapp.org/directadmissions.

23. Mary Churchill, "The SAT and ACT Are Less Important Than You Might Think," *Inside Higher Ed,* January 29, 2023. https://www.insidehighered.com/blogs/higher-ed-policy/sat-and-act-are-less-important-you-might-think.

24. Michelle Miller-Adams, *The Path to Free College: In Pursuit of Access, Equity, and Prosperity* (Cambridge, MA: Harvard Education Press, 2021).

25. Massachusetts Department of Elementary and Secondary Education, Early College Promise (ECP) Pilot Program, accessed May 3, 2024.

26. CollegePromise.org, https://www.collegepromise.org/.

27. "Community College FAQs," Community College Research Center, accessed May 5, 2024. https://ccrc.tc.columbia.edu/community-college-faqs.html.

28. Jill Barshay, "Proof Points: High Schoolers Account for Nearly 1 out of Every 5 Community College Students," Hechinger Report, July 24. 2023. https://hechingerreport.org/proof-points-high-schoolers-account-for-nearly-1-out-of-every-5-community-college-students/.

29. Sarah Goldrick-Rab, *Paying the Price: College Costs, Financial Aid, and the Betrayal of the American Dream* (Chicago: University of Chicago Press, 2016).

30. Michelle R. Weise, *Long Life Learning: Preparing for Jobs That Don't Even Exist Yet.* (Hoboken, NJ: Wiley and Sons, 2020).

31. Simpson, *Longing for Justice,* 40

The Conversation on Higher Ed

Part I.

Succeeding at College

For students and their families, applying to college has gotten far more complicated. This is especially the case for those high school students seeking a full-time, residential college experience—what we tend to call the "traditional" college experience. As Poynton points out, in his chapter of part I, the increasing expense of a college education has intensified the pressure on many students and their families to apply to and get into the "right" college. With the price of an undergraduate college degree sometimes equal to or greater than the price of a family home, the stakes are high. Often students and their families spend months, if not years, creating lists of reach, target, and safety schools; attending in-person and virtual junior visit days; and spending the summer before senior year finalizing their lists.

Parents often help their students through the process, and most high schools have programs and staff who assist students with creating lists and drafting application essays. During the COVID-19 pandemic, most universities went test optional. Some institutions have since reinstated SAT or ACT requirements for admission, yet many have continued to be test optional. Additionally, the practice of direct admissions has been increasingly implemented by states. In direct admissions, often administered at the state level, offers of admission are sent to students to either accept or decline. For students who do not see themselves as college-going or lack the confidence to apply, the practice of direct admissions removes some of the doubt.

The chapters in part I highlight some of the issues that are crucial for students as they work to set themselves up for success. The opening chapters, from Poynton and Churchill, focus on the preparation required of students to gain admission to a college that is a good fit for them. The following chapters offer guidance on how to succeed in college once enrolled, including excellent advice on how to approach student loans from Nguyen, Smith, and Chan and from Wendler. Success in college requires more than being financially savvy, and Lambert, Artze-Vega, Miranda Tapia, and Felten stress that relationships are key to student mental health. The college experience can be a lonely one, especially for students who have moved far away from home to attend college. Completing college successfully is often tied to establishing meaningful relationships with peers and mentors. One of the best ways to build these relationships is through internships and on-campus employment, but Ecton, Heinrich, and Carruthers caution that working off campus for more than 15 hours a week can impede students' ability to finish their degree on time.

By looking closely at the work done to support students' successful transitions from high school to college, we begin to see how creating deeper partnerships between colleges and universities and their local public-school districts can lead to increased student success, while also having the potential to reverse the declining college demand curve.

Chapter 1

4 Tips for Choosing a Good College— and Getting Accepted

TIMOTHY POYNTON, *University of Massachusetts, Boston*

WITH MORE THAN 2,800 FOUR-YEAR colleges and universities in the United States, finding the one that is right for you can feel overwhelming. The task can be particularly hard for high school students who are the first in their family to attend college—commonly referred to as first-generation students.[1]

In my experience as a professor and researcher focused on how to improve the transition from high school to college, I have found that there is a significant "college knowledge

First-generation college students have less "college knowledge" than students whose parents went to college.
SDI Productions / E+ via Getty Images

gap" between first-generation college students and students whose parents went to college.

Given the ever-rising costs of a college education, the stakes for finding the right college are high. With that in mind, here are four tips that can help first-generation college students not only get into the college of their choice but also secure scholarship money to help pay for it.

1. Look Up How Students Do After They Graduate

If you want to see your odds of getting into a particular school, how much it will cost, or what percentage of students graduate from the school each year, the federal government has several websites that track those things. One website is called the Integrated Postsecondary Education Data System, or IPEDS. More user-friendly websites include the College Navigator and the College Scorecard. The College Scorecard provides information on how much student loan debt and what kind of salary you can expect after graduation. This information can be found for particular majors.

If you see that a low percentage of students from a school graduate, you may want to ask an admissions representative at the school if they have updated information. The data on graduation rates available on the federal websites is based on students who started as freshmen at the school seven to nine years ago. You may also want to consider a different school. Similarly, you may want to explore other colleges if you see that graduates from one school have more debts or lower salaries than most other graduates.

2. Do Well in Challenging High School Classes

The single best thing you can do to increase your chances of getting into your dream college is to take the most challenging classes available at your high school and do as well as possible in those classes.

This will also help you get scholarship money, as many colleges award merit scholarships based in part on your high school grade point average. Doing well in your classes is more important than admission test scores. According to an annual survey of college admissions directors, GPA has been more important than SAT or ACT test scores since long before the COVID-19 pandemic.[2]

3. Show Your Interest

In addition to reviewing your transcript, colleges also consider various nonacademic factors. Of course, this includes things like extracurricular activities and volunteer experience. But more than four out of five colleges also look at something called "demonstrated interest."

Perhaps the strongest way to demonstrate interest in a college is by applying early decision to your first-choice college. When you apply early decision, you are committing to attend the college if you are accepted. The only ethical reason for turning down an early decision offer is if attending the college is not affordable for you and your family. Another way to demonstrate interest in a college is by visiting the college's campus and taking a tour. You may also participate in an optional admissions interview, follow the college on social media, and read and respond to email messages sent by the college.

If you follow a college on social media, be sure there is nothing on your account that could hurt your chances of being admitted. Some students have had college offers rescinded as a result of things they posted online.

4. Organize Information to Do Comparisons

Once you gather information you think is important about each college, such as graduation rates, interesting majors, and how much tuition will cost after you get financial aid, organize it in table form in a spreadsheet so that you can do a visual comparison. If you're not into making spreadsheets, the College Navigator allows you to "favorite" schools for comparison. Similarly, the College Scorecard allows you to "compare" information side by side for schools you choose.

Whatever method you choose, be sure to do the comparisons again after you get your acceptance letters, which should detail how much financial aid or scholarship money you are offered to defray the cost of attendance. The comparisons will be even more crucial as you get closer to making your final choice.

It's natural to have preconceptions about schools. For instance, you might be enamored with the school's football team or have heard that it is a great place to party. By taking the time to do a little homework about the colleges you may want to attend, you'll have some objective information to go along with whatever thoughts and feelings you have about a given school.

Notes

1. Timothy A. Poynton, Richard T. Lapan, and Sophie W. Schuyler, "Reducing Inequality in High School Students' College Knowledge: The Role of School Counselors," *Professional School Counseling* 24, no. 1, pt. 3 (May 2021). https://doi.org/10.1177/2156759x211011894.
2. "Factors in the Admission Decision" (for fall 2023 admission cycle), National Association for College Admission Counseling. https://www.nacacnet.org/factors-in-the-admission-decision/.

Chapter 2

The SAT and ACT Are Less Important Than You Might Think

MARY L. CHURCHILL, *Boston University*

COLLEGE ADMISSION TESTS are becoming a thing of the past.

More than 80% of US colleges and universities do not require applicants to take standardized tests—like the SAT or the ACT—as of early 2024. The proportion of institutions with test-optional policies more than doubled since spring 2020. And in the fall of 2023, some 85 institutions didn't even consider standardized test scores when reviewing applications. That includes the entire University of California system. Only 4% of colleges that use the

Common Application system required a standardized test for admission.

Even before the COVID-19 pandemic, more than 1,000 colleges and universities had either test-optional or so-called test-blind policies, but as the pandemic unfolded, more than 600 additional institutions followed suit. At the time, many college officials noted that health concerns and other logistics associated with test taking made them want to reduce student stress and risk. Concerns about racial equity also factored in many of these decisions.

Other institutions are what some call "test-flexible," allowing applicants to submit test scores from Advanced Placement or International Baccalaureate exams in place of the SAT or ACT.

Tests under Fire

For many years, some educators have fought against the use of standardized tests, in general, and for college admission in particular.

One critique is simple: standardized tests aren't that useful at measuring a student's academic potential. Research has repeatedly shown that a student's grade point average in high school is a better predictor of college success than standardized test scores on the SAT or ACT.[1]

But there are deeper issues, too, involving race and equity.

The development and use of standardized tests in higher education came out of the eugenics movement. That movement claimed—and then used misleading and manufactured evidence to support the idea—that people of different races had different innate abilities. "Standardized tests have become the most effective racist weapon ever devised to objectively degrade Black and Brown minds and legally exclude their bodies from prestigious schools," argues Ibram X. Kendi, director of the Center for Antiracist Research at Boston University.[2]

Kendi is not alone in highlighting the historical links between standardized tests and discrimination. Joseph A. Soares, editor of *The Scandal of Standardized Tests: Why We Need to Drop the SAT and ACT*, writes, "[t]he original ugly eugenic racist intention behind the SAT, aimed at excluding Jews from the Ivy League." He says that this same exclusionary goal has now "been realized by biased test-question selection algorithms that systemically discriminate against Blacks."[3] In his work, Soares draws attention to the practice of evaluating pilot questions and removing from the final version of the test those questions on which Black students did better than white students.

My colleague Joshua Goodman has found that Black and Latino students who take the SAT or the ACT are less likely than white or Asian students to take it a second time. They perform less well, which contributes to disproportionately low representation of college students from low-income and racial-minority backgrounds.[4]

Those factors—as well as a lawsuit claiming discrimination based on test performance—were behind the May 2020 decision by the University of California's Board of Regents to discontinue using SAT and ACT scores in admissions decisions.

Economics of Higher Education

Colleges and universities seek applicants with good grades and other achievements, and they want a diverse pool from which to build their classes. Colleges that did not require standardized tests in applications for students arriving in fall 2021 "generally received more applicants, better academically qualified applicants, and more diverse pools of applicants."[5] That's according to Bob Schaeffer, executive director of FairTest, an advocacy group working to "end the misuses and flaws of testing practices" in K–12 and higher education.

In addition, birth rates are declining, and the number of 18-year-olds seeking to enter college is decreasing. Many institutions are trying to make it easier for people to apply to college.

As a result of these factors, I expect to see high school students begin to choose where to apply based at least in part on whether colleges require standardized tests, consider them, or ignore them entirely. According to *U.S. News & World Report*, most of the colleges in the United States that still require test scores are located in southern states, with the highest count in the state of Florida.

The Testing Business

The test-taking business, including preparatory classes, tutoring, and test registration fees, is a multibillion-dollar industry.

As more institutions reduce their attention to tests, all those businesses feel pressure to reinvent themselves and make their services useful. The College Board, which produces the SAT and other tests, has recently tried to make its flagship test more "student-friendly," as the organization put it. In January 2022 it released an online SAT that is supposed to be easier for test sites to administer and easier for students to take.

In recent conversations I have had in researching higher education policies, admission directors at selective universities tell me that standardized test scores have become an optional component of a portfolio of activities, awards, and other material that applicants have at their disposal when completing their college applications.

Institutions that have gone test-blind have already decided that the SAT is no longer part of the equation. Others may join them.

Dartmouth, Brown, Yale, the Massachusetts Institute of Technology, and a few other elite institutions announced that they were reinstating mandatory standardized testing, and, suddenly, the SAT and ACT were in the news cycle again. The overwhelming majority of colleges and universities in the United States, however, are broad-access institutions that do not require a standardized test score as part of their application; therefore, for most US college students, this is a nonissue.

Notes

1. Elaine M. Allensworth and Kallie Clark, "High School GPAs and ACT Scores as Predictors of College Completion: Examining Assumptions about Consistency across High Schools," *Educational Researcher* 49, no. 3 (January 27, 2020): 198–211. https://doi.org/10.3102/0013189 x20902110.
2. "Public Statement by Ibram X. Kendi," Boston Coalition for Education Equity, October 21, 2020. https://www.bosedequity.org/blog/read -ibram-x-kendis-testimony-in-support-of-the-working-group -recommendation-to-suspendthetest.
3. Joseph A. Soares, "Dismantling White Supremacy Includes Ending Racist Tests like the SAT and ACT," Teachers College Press blog, June 22, 2020. https://www.tcpress.com/blog/dismantling-white -supremacy-includes-racist-tests-sat-act/.
4. Joshua Goodman, Oded Gurantz, and Jonathan Smith, "Take Two! SAT Retaking and College Enrollment Gaps," *American Economic*

Journal: Economic Policy 12, no. 2 (May 2020): 115–58. https://doi.org /10.1257/pol.20170503.

5. Quoted in Shirin Ali, "Harvard Ditching Standardized Testing Requirements for Admissions for Next Four Years," The Hill, December 17, 2021. https://thehill.com/changing-america/enrichment /education/586321-harvard-ditching-standardized-testing -requirements-for/.

Chapter 3

How Direct Admission Is Changing the Process of Applying for College

MARY L. CHURCHILL, *Boston University*

FOR STUDENTS AND THEIR FAMILIES who are considering college, a relatively new option for admission is gaining popularity. In addition to the long-standing process of regular admission, and various options for early admission decisions, is something called *direct admission*. Direct admission is one of several strategies that colleges and universities use to make it easier for high school graduates to go to college. They are also hoping it can help reverse a trend of declining enrollment in higher education in the United States.[1]

What Is Direct Admission?

In direct admission, soon-to-be high school graduates can be accepted into a college or university without having to submit an application. This often happens during a student's senior year of high school, but some colleges make these offers during junior year.

Applying to college can take a lot of money and time and requires that students figure out the college application process, which can sometimes be complex.[2] The fear of rejection also discourages some people from applying. With direct admission, this fear of rejection is removed because qualified students receive an acceptance letter from a college without needing to apply.

How Can Students Qualify?

In some cases, all a student has to do is graduate from high school. In other cases, students have to achieve a certain GPA or score on the ACT or SAT.

Students don't typically know that they have qualified until they receive an acceptance letter. Many community colleges are charged with offering educational opportunities to any member of the public. So many are directly admitting all students who graduate from a given high school or district. Other colleges are more selective and may admit all graduates with grades or standardized test scores above a minimum.

In some states, all students who graduate from a public high school are offered admission to a set of public colleges and universities in that state. Idaho was the first to do this, in 2015.

What Are the Benefits for Colleges?

A big advantage for direct admission for institutions is that they get direct access to the students they want to attract, which may differ from school to school. Often the most desirable students are top scholars, people from a particular geographic area, or those having some combination of demographic attributes, like racial or ethnic background or family economic status. Having this access enables colleges to reach more students than they could if they only reached students through high school visits and college fairs and direct marketing.

In addition, a college has an opportunity to reach potential students from more demographically diverse backgrounds than their usual applicants. For example, colleges can target high schools with a lot of students from a particular group that is underrepresented on their campus and that they hope to attract. They can offer direct admission to all qualifying students in a school's graduating class.

If a college wants to enroll more male students, it could offer direct admission to those attending all-boys high schools. If it wants to enroll more Black and Latino males, it could offer direct admission to those at all-boys high schools with large populations of Black and Latino students.

What Are the Benefits for Students?

Direct admission does not require students or their families to fill out an application or pay an application fee. Of course, students who accept the offer must complete paperwork and pay tuition and other costs associated with enrolling—but they need not do anything to receive an admission offer from the college.

When an unexpected acceptance letter arrives from a well-known college, it can help students who didn't see college in their future begin to envision themselves as a college student. Some colleges target students for direct admission even earlier than their junior year because they know that students often decide whether they want to go to college as early as middle school.

Evidence shows that direct admission programs lead to more students admitted to colleges and to more students attending. When Idaho launched its statewide direct admissions program in 2015, overall college enrollment grew by about 8%.[3]

Is This the Future of College Admissions?

For colleges that are nonselective, direct admission has a lot of potential. It is a relatively inexpensive way for an individual college, or an entire state, to make college opportunities more clearly available to more students. Colleges can get the attention of their desired student populations.

As direct admission becomes more common, colleges—especially community colleges—will likely need additional staff and money to handle a growth in admissions. Some institutions are partnering with education management companies, such as Concourse, Sage Solutions, and the Common Application. These institutions may be able to spend less on marketing and recruitment over time. Initially, though, they will need to spend more to process students who are admitted directly.

Students may find themselves receiving admission letters from colleges they've never applied to—and perhaps never even heard of. This may lead students to turn more to guidance counselors to help them decide which direct admission offer to accept based on a school's cost, academic programs, and other factors.

Notes

1. Nathan D. Grawe, *The Agile College: How Institutions Successfully Navigate Demographic Changes* (Baltimore: Johns Hopkins University Press, 2021).
2. Scott Carrell and Bruce Sacerdote, "Why Do College-Going Interventions Work?," *American Economic Journal: Applied Economics* 9, no. 3 (July 1, 2017): 124–51. https://doi.org/10.1257/app.20150530.
3. Taylor K. Odle and Jennifer A. Delaney. "You Are Admitted! Early Evidence on Enrollment from Idaho's Direct Admissions System," *Research in Higher Education* 63, no. 6 (2022): 899–932.

Chapter 4

5 Things to Consider before Taking Out a Student Loan

DAVID J. NGUYEN, *Ohio University*

KATIE N. SMITH, *Temple University*

MONNICA CHAN, *University of Massachusetts, Boston*

15.9 MILLION.

That's how many students enrolled in college at the undergraduate level in fall 2020. Of that number, about 38% were awarded federal student loans.[1] Taking out loans is a decision that could bring certain rewards—not least of which is a well-paying job—but that can also come with serious economic consequences you should understand.

Among borrowers, the average federal student loan debt for graduates in the class of 2020 was an estimated US$30,500.[2] Not everyone is able to make steady payments on their student loans. Prior to the COVID-19 pandemic and temporary policies of student loan repayment relief, 7.3% of student loan borrowers who entered repayment in 2018 had defaulted on their loan repayments by 2020.[3]

As researchers who specialize in how money shapes the way people make education decisions, we have five tips for students and families who are thinking about how to pay for college.

1. File for Federal Aid Early

Though this may seem like common practice among college-goers, more than two million people do not file the Free Application for Federal Student Aid, better known as the FAFSA. Sometimes parents and students don't know about this form. Some parents may be unwilling to provide their tax return information, which is used to determine eligibility for student aid. Some people may start the form but never complete it. The FAFSA matters.

Filing the FAFSA is required to determine eligibility for federal student aid programs. It can be particularly important for students whose families have little or no money to pay for college. In these cases, students may be eligible for a federal Pell Grant, which is awarded to students with significant financial need and does not have to be paid back. Filing the FAFSA may also be required for other financial aid that students could get from the state or the college they plan to attend.

The FAFSA Simplification Act requires that the US Department of Education roll out a simplified FAFSA form for the 2024–25 academic year. The simplified FAFSA is shorter and draws federal tax information directly from the Internal Revenue Service, with student or parental consent. Most students and families will now be able to apply in minutes for federal financial aid. While the rollout of the new FAFSA faced some hurdles in late 2023 and early 2024 (the time of this writing), the form should be available as early as October 2024 for the 2025–26 academic year. Financial aid applicants can start the process by creating an account at StudentAid.gov. Applying for student financial aid as early as possible can help forestall any administrative complications. Applying early is also important given the varying deadlines for state and institutional financial aid programs that rely on the FAFSA.

2. Understand Different Types of Loans

Different loan options include federal loans, private loans from banks, or credit cards.

Federal loans are typically your best option. This is because federal loans often have low fixed interest rates. Federal loans also have provisions for deferment, a time period when your loans do not accrue interest. They offer a grace period before the repayment period begins and forbearance, which is a time period of postponed repayment for those who can demonstrate hardship in making payments. During forbearance, though, your student loan balance continues to accrue interest. Federal loans also come with various repayment programs, such as income-based repayment.

You may have options for subsidized and unsubsidized loans. Subsidized loans are funded by the government and offer better interest rate terms. They are based on need and do not accrue interest while you are still in school. Unsubsidized loans may be available regardless of your financial need, but they accrue interest as soon as the loan is distributed to you. In other words, the minute you accept the promissory note for the loan, you will owe interest.

Private loans tend to have higher interest rates, although rates for these loans and for credit cards can fluctuate. Private loans do not allow for participation in government repayment programs.

3. Contact Your Financial Aid Adviser

Call the financial aid office to figure out who is your assigned financial aid adviser at the school you plan to attend. This person will be able to help you better understand your institutional aid package.

Be sure to review the different sources of aid listed in your financial aid award letter. Some sources of aid may be institutional grant aid, which is financial aid offered by the college you plan to attend. Other sources include federal loans and federal work-study. Federal work-study is neither a grant nor a loan. Instead, this program allows students to defray education expenses by working on campus.

Some schools package loans, such as Parent PLUS loans, directly as part of the offer to you and your family.

4. Understand the Impact of Debt

Taking out loans for college can be an investment in your future, especially when loan money allows you to work less and focus more on coursework to complete your degree in a timely manner. Research consistently shows that a college degree is worth the cost. On average, college graduates earn far more over the course of their career than their peers who didn't get a college degree.

Students taking out loans should be conscious, however, of how much they are borrowing. Many students do not know how much they owe or how student loan debt works.

You may access the National Student Loan Data System to learn more about your personal federal loans. Over one million borrowers in the United States are currently in default on their student loans after they failed to make monthly payments for a period of about nine months. Defaulting on student loans can have serious consequences. It can prevent you from receiving financial aid in the future. The federal government may garnish a portion of your wages or withhold your tax refund. You can also lose eligibility for loan deferment and forbearance and ruin your credit score.

Taking on a significant amount of debt can have other long-term implications. For instance, debt can hurt your ability to purchase a home or move out of your parents' home into an apartment.

5. Know Your Repayment Options

In thinking about your repayment options, there are many factors that may influence how much money you make after college, including your major and career path. Since your future salary can influence your ability to pay back loans, it is important for borrowers to have a sense of earnings across different fields and industries. Yet many college students do not have an accurate idea of how much money they can expect to earn in the careers they are considering, although this information can be found in the federal government's online Occupational Outlook Handbook.[4]

There are several options designed to help borrowers repay their loans, including payment plans based on income level and programs of loan forgiveness.

To make loan payments more manageable based on your income, consider an income-driven repayment plan based on your loan type and financial situation. Borrowers need to apply for income-driven repayment plans. Income-driven repayment plans allow borrowers to pay somewhere between 5% and 20% of their discretionary income toward their student loans each month, rather than the predetermined payment based on loan size.

Borrowers might also research loan forgiveness programs offered by their state or for certain professions. Programs may be available that provide students funding while in college or that forgive a portion of loans if graduates enter jobs where qualified individuals are needed, such as the teaching profession.

Another option might be the Public Service Loan Forgiveness program offered by the federal government to students working in public service jobs, such as teaching or nonprofit organizations.

Notes

1. "Loans for Undergraduate Students and Debt for Bachelor's Degree Recipients," National Center for Education Statistics, May 2023. https://nces.ed.gov/programs/coe/indicator/cub.
2. "Digest of Education Statistics," Table 331.95, National Center for Education Statistics, 2023. https://nces.ed.gov/programs/digest/d23/tables/dt23_331.95.asp.

3. "Digest of Education Statistics, 2022," Table 332.50, National Center for Education Statistics, 2023. https://nces.ed.gov/programs/digest /d22/tables/dt22_332.50.asp.
4. See the US Bureau of Labor Statistics, https://www.bls.gov/ooh/home .htm.

Chapter 5

A College President's Advice to College Students of the Future Is Don't Borrow

WALTER V. WENDLER, *West Texas A&M University*

BACK IN 2017, I started regularly leaving my office at West Texas A&M University in Canyon, Texas, to speak to high school students in the Texas Panhandle. In the fall of 2019, I did the same thing in the South Plains. These two areas contain the 46 northernmost counties in the state of Texas.

Driving a silver SUV owned by the university, I logged a total of 14,000 miles throughout these two regions over a total of 10 months. I visited 132 high schools with student populations of all sizes. For instance, in the South Plains tour, I visited 66 schools that ranged in size from Lubbock High School, where I spoke to 975 juniors and seniors, to Dawson High School, where I spoke with all 12 high school students in ninth through twelfth grades.

No matter where I went—and no matter whether I spoke with students and families that had a concrete plan for college or those that were less certain—I heard concerns about the cost of higher education. My message and response was always the same: "Do not borrow money to attend West Texas A&M University, or any university, for the first two years. If you must borrow to attend a university, then attend community college first, but don't borrow a penny for community college either. Pay as you go."

In deciding whether to start higher education in junior college, use side-by-side cost comparisons. Honest and transparent assessment may show that direct entry into a senior, or four-year, institution is cost effective when financial aid, grants, scholarships, cost-of-living, and transfer credit losses are carefully assessed. The old adage holds. Buyer beware. And I should have added this: live with your parents rent-free as long as possible.

Planning for the Future

You might think I was simply on a recruiting tour for the university where I serve as president. Yes, of course, I hoped my visits would make my university more appealing. My primary purpose, however, was not recruiting students but was instead helping them determine a long-range plan toward becoming what I call "noble citizens," who are ready to work, engage, think, and vote.

You can become a noble citizen and still carry a lot of debt. It's just a lot more difficult to do. If you are saddled with debt, you're less able to contribute to your community, at least financially, or purchase a home. As I spoke with students, I shared a few statistics to help illustrate the point.

Fifty-four percent of college students graduated with debt in 2023—amounting, on average, to US$30,000.[1] Some of those graduates will still be paying off their student loans decades later when they get Social Security checks, either voluntarily or by having those checks garnished. Of Americans over 60 years old, 3.5 million have student loans. Forty-two percent of those are cosigners paying for the loans of children or grandchildren, but the rest are students paying off their own education loans.[2]

A growing number of aging Americans have college debt that they will not pay back before dying. Default rates for borrowers over 65 are nearly 35%, according to the Consumer Financial Protection Bureau.[3]

Pell Grants, which are federal grants to help low-income students pay for college, covered 79% of tuition and fees in 1975 but only covered 14.8% by 2024,[4] a downhill slide caused by escalating tuition and easy loans.

Mixed Results for Borrowing

Some studies suggest that borrowing yields an increase in college credits earned and academic performance. Despite those benefits, other research shows that carrying student loan debt can have a negative long-term effect on people financially and emotionally.

On my tour, I told students, if they must borrow, never to borrow more than 60% of their anticipated starting salary in their first postgraduation job. This is consistent with what I call the "60% Rule," which a state agency of higher education developed to counsel students not to borrow more than their degree is worth.

For example, if someone wanted to teach school in a small Texas community for a $40,000 starting salary, they should not borrow more than $24,000 to attain a bachelor's degree. Similar—although more lenient—advice comes from *Forbes*, which urged borrowers never to borrow more than they expected to make from their salary the first year of employment.[5] (For information about the expected salary for a particular job, check out the US Bureau of Labor Statistics.)

In urging students not to take on too much student debt, I also highlighted other paths—aside from college—to noble citizenship: military service, certification programs, or family-run businesses.

A Duty to Inform

I recognize the responsibility of university leadership to point out the challenges for students and families when borrowing for education. It is difficult for middle-income families to pay the increasing costs of a college education. Informed borrowing is the key issue for students. The need is highlighted for students who are first in their family to attend college and who may accept the claim that any college degree is worth whatever it costs. It is not true. And it is an unfair burden for university leadership to place on students.

If students do borrow for college, they should be aware that they are possibly being sucked into what I like to call a troubling triangle of treachery.

One side of the triangle is represented by elected officials who encourage everyone to go to college. The second side is represented by lenders, who—in my view—do little to assess an individual's ability to repay a student loan. If a student borrows to enroll in a college, the limits placed on amounts borrowed are quite high when federal and private loans are combined. Lenders tend to treat all college degrees and, by inference, employment opportunities as equal. Yet the employment marketplace reveals that this is not the case. The third side is represented by university leadership, which—in my view—has not done enough to let students know the pitfalls of borrowing.

Students' indebtedness is eventually their own responsibility. Debt responsibility will not disappear for them—or the parents who are helping them. It's their parents' responsibility too. Just ask the 44 million Americans, many of whom did not graduate, who collectively owe an estimated US$1.5 trillion in student loan debt.

My tour of northern Texas counties was a learning experience. The value proposition of American higher education is changing. I saw it in the eyes of 20,000 students across 14,000 miles.

Notes

1. Heidi Rivera, "Student Loan Debt Statistics," Bankrate, December 13, 2023. https://www.bankrate.com/loans/student-loans/student-loan-debt-statistics/.
2. Tia Caldwell, Rachel Fishman, and Sarah Sattelmeyer, "Older Americans with Student Loan Debt," New America, December 11, 2023. https://www.newamerica.org/education-policy/collections/older-americans-with-student-loan-debt/.
3. Annie Nova, "Another Challenge in Retirement? Student Loans," CNBC, November 14, 2018. https://www.cnbc.com/2018/11/14/more

-older-people-are-bringing-student-debt-into-their-retirement
.html.

4. Melanie Hanson, "Pell Grant Statistics," Education Data Initiative,
January 28, 2024. https://educationdata.org/pell-grant-statistics.

5. Jason Lina, "When Does Student Debt Make Sense, and When Doesn't
It?," *Forbes*, October 14, 2019. https://www.forbes.com/sites/law
rencelight/2019/10/04/when-does-student-debt-make-sense-and
-when-doesnt-it/?sh=902583413703.

Chapter 6

Building Relationships Is Key for First-Year College Students

Here Are 5 Easy Ways to Meet New Friends and Mentors

LEO M. LAMBERT, *Elon University*

ISIS ARTZE-VEGA, *Valencia College*

OSCAR R. MIRANDA TAPIA, *North Carolina State University*

PETER FELTEN, *Elon University*

WHAT'S THE BEST ADVICE we can give to a new college student? Connections are everything.

Research for decades has shown that the relationships students cultivate in college—with professors, staff, and fellow students—are key to success. Simply put, human connections matter for learning and well-being in college; they also set students up for professional and personal fulfillment after they graduate.

College students confirmed the importance of connections when we interviewed more than 250 of them at three dozen colleges and universities throughout the United States for our book *Connections Are Everything: A College Student's Guide to Relationship-Rich Education*.[1]

Although no two students had the same story to tell, what they told us was surprisingly similar—and it reinforced the research on the power of relationships. What can college students do to harness the power of relationships to support their academic success and personal well-being? Here are five steps recommended by students and scholars.

1. Talk to a Professor

The quality and frequency of student-faculty interactions play a major role in learning.[2] Approaching a faculty member can feel intimidating, but it can be done in simple ways.

Introduce yourself before or after class. Visit during your professor's in-person or online office hours, which is time set aside for students to meet with their professor. You don't need to connect with every professor right away. Start with one in the first week of the term. You can seek help in or guidance about the class, or you can ask the professor about their professional background.

José Robles, a nursing student at Nevada State College, told us about being surprised at the connections he built with a professor in a required science course that he thought would be "as boring as rocks." This professor's teaching inspired him to love geology—and to get excited about learning in general.

José's experience is not unusual. A national poll of college graduates found that 60% met their most influential faculty mentor in college during their first year.[3]

2. Make a Friend in Class

First-year students often feel alone in big introductory courses and in online classes, but those can be opportunities to connect with students who will help you succeed.

Chloe Inskeep, a first-generation college student at the University of Iowa, told us about her strategy for making connections, even when her classes had almost as many students as the population of her hometown: "Lots of students go to class, and then they leave or log out as soon as it ends. For me, just staying after a little bit to chat with other people really helps me find people who I have something in common with."

Research shows that students who study together tend to do better academically than students who study alone.[4] They also tend to be less stressed by their classes. A guide from the Learning Center at the University of North Carolina at Chapel Hill recommends that students form small groups of committed individuals who meet at least once weekly, whether online or on campus.

3. Use the Resources That Are There for You

Colleges have many programs and offices to support student learning, development, and well-being. These range from writing and tutoring programs to student organizations, counseling centers, and resource hubs for students who identify as LGBTQ+, first-generation, students of color, or who have a disability.

Mirella Cisneros Perez met both welcoming peers and a critical mentor, Dean Sylvia Munoz, after a friend introduced her to the Latinx/Hispanic Union at Elon University. "Whenever I would run into them, I knew they believed in me and wanted me to succeed," Mirella told us. "The connections my peers guided me to helped me find my place at Elon and changed my whole experience in college for the positive."

Like Mirella, many students we interviewed said a college staff member was their most important first connection on campus. Even one relationship like this can contribute to your success—a first step in building a "constellation of mentors," the people who will support and challenge you productively in every dimension of your life.[5]

4. Participate in a Relationship Accelerator

Relationship accelerator is the term we use to describe powerful college experiences that help students integrate classroom learning with real-world experiences and human connections.[6] These experiences include internships, undergraduate research, writing-intensive seminars, study abroad, and even campus employment.

For example, your campus job supervisor can help you learn valuable new skills and can challenge you to integrate your paid work with your academic learning. Peta Gaye Dixon, a student at LaGuardia Community College in New York City, told us that her campus job supervisor "sees stuff in me that I don't see in myself."

5. Connect with Yourself

New students often experience a bit of imposter syndrome—feeling like you might not be as smart or qualified as other students. That's completely normal, and it's something that you can work through.

Don't lose sight of who you are and the many strengths you bring with you to college. If a bump in the road has you feeling anxious—if, say, you don't do as well as you had hoped on that first quiz—talk to a professor, tutor, or friend. We met Joshua Rodriguez, a student at Oakton Community College near Chicago, who considered dropping his Calculus 2 class until his professor advised him to read up on imposter syndrome instead of doing the homework one night.

That opened Joshua's eyes: "That interaction bolstered my confidence to realize that I'm not alone in this, that everyone has these feelings," he said. "I went from contemplating dropping out to getting tutoring help—and then getting an A in the course." Joshua ultimately earned a bachelor's degree in nuclear engineering from Purdue University.

Trusting yourself—and challenging yourself—is vital to your success in school and in life. We promise that if you pursue meaningful relationships, you'll be setting yourself up well to thrive in college.

Notes

1. Peter Felten, Leo M. Lambert, Isis Artze-Vega, and Oscar R. Miranda Tapia, *Connections Are Everything: A College Student's Guide to Relationship-Rich Education* (Baltimore: Johns Hopkins University Press, 2023). The book is available in an open-access edition that is free to download at https://muse.jhu.edu/book/111986.
2. Carol A. Lundberg and Laurie A. Schreiner, "Quality and Frequency of Faculty-Student Interaction as Predictors of Learning: An Analysis by Student Race/Ethnicity," *Journal of College Student Development* 45, no. 5 (2004): 549–65. https://doi.org/10.1353/csd.2004.0061.
3. Leo M. Lambert, Jason Husser, and Peter Felten, "Mentors Play Critical Role in Quality of College Experience, New Poll Suggests,"

The Conversation, August 22, 2018. https://theconversation.com /mentors-play-critical-role-in-quality-of-college-experience-new -poll-suggests-101861.

4. Uri Treisman, "Studying Students Studying Calculus: A Look at the Lives of Minority Mathematics Students in College," *College Mathematics Journal* 23, no. 5 (November 1992): 362–72. https://doi.org/10 .1080/07468342.1992.11973486.

5. W. Brad Johnson, *On Being a Mentor: A Guide for Higher Education Faculty*, 2nd ed. (New York: Routledge, 2015).

6. Center for Engaged Learning at Elon University, *Relationship Accelerators—Connections Are Everything*, YouTube video, posted July 21, 2023. https://www.youtube.com/watch?v=_VQOLXICEuU&t =33s.

Chapter 7

Advanced Degrees Bring Higher Starting Salaries—but Also Higher Debt

JAYMES PYNE, *Stanford University*

ERIC GRODSKY, *University of Wisconsin, Madison*

PEOPLE WITH A MASTER'S DEGREE or doctorate can bank on a much higher starting salary than those with the same major but only a bachelor's degree. That's according to a 2020 survey of employers by the National Association of Colleges and Employers.[1] We reached the same conclusion about the payoff for advanced degrees in a study of ours published in a 2019.[2] As sociologists who study inequality and disadvantage in education, we also know that the picture becomes more complicated when you see how different kinds of students pay for school.

Salary and Debt Comparisons

The results of the association's 2020 survey suggest that a person with a master's degree in math, science, engineering, computer science, or business can expect a starting salary between US$75,000 and US$79,000 a year for a job in their field. Those starting salaries are 10% to 30% higher than projected starting salaries for the typical person with a bachelor's degree with a similar job.

Starting salaries are even higher for those graduating with a doctoral degree. For example, the average American with a PhD in engineering, math, or science could expect to make slightly over US$100,000 a year once they complete their degree, while those leaving college with a bachelor's degree in the same fields could expect to start out making between US$62,500 and US$70,000 a year.

We call this gap an "advanced degree wage premium." It's the increased amount of money that college graduates who go on to earn a master's, doctoral, or professional degree in law, medicine, and other fields can expect to make above those with just a bachelor's degree.

We also found, though, that Americans who continue their studies after earning their baccalaureate degree tend to borrow more for their undergraduate education than those who do not.

We determined that the typical college student who needs to borrow money for their undergraduate studies and ends their formal education after college takes out roughly US$13,500 in loans. With a constant 6% interest rate, it would cost US$500 a month for two and a half years to pay off that amount of debt.

Borrowers who get graduate degrees, on the other hand, typically borrow roughly US$25,000 as undergraduates. Some then accumulate even more student loan debt on top of that in graduate school. A student pursuing a graduate degree typically takes out another US$35,000 after completing undergraduate studies. With a US$500-per-month payment plan and a constant 6% interest rate, someone taking out US$25,000 in loans would take nearly 5 years to pay off their debt, while a graduate student taking out US$70,000 in loans would take 20 years to fully repay them.

Amounts of debt vary by degree program. For example, 51% of those with a master of business administration (MBA) who borrowed money for their education and finished business school in 2016 owed an average of US$66,300. Grads who earned a doctorate in science or engineering, psychology, business or public administration, or fine arts or theology and who borrowed to pay for their education owed about twice as much: US$132,000. Given a US$1,000 monthly payment with a constant 6% interest rate compounded monthly, it would take roughly 6 years to pay off the principal and interest for the typical MBA amount versus 18 years to pay off the principal and interest of a typical doctorate degree.

These debt burdens, moreover, are not borne equally by all.

In the starkest example, we found that African Americans who go to graduate school tend to borrow about 50% more than white students with similar degrees. Under certain conditions, African American graduate student borrowers could take 11 years longer to pay off their loans than typical white graduate student borrowers. African Americans earning master's degrees see an average 30% jump in salaries compared with African Americans with bachelor's degrees in similar fields. And African Americans see a 65% increase in their salaries above their peers with only a bachelor's degree if they earn a PhD or similar degree. Those salary jumps are 12 and 10 percentage points higher than their white counterparts, respectively.

The Bigger Picture

Americans currently owe more than US$1.7 trillion in student loan debt. Yes, getting an MBA, a law degree, or similar credentials usually increases earnings, but there are also economic, social, and psychological costs associated with racking up all the student loan debt it takes to get there. For example, those costs could include deferring investing for retirement, starting a family, or buying a house as well as the anxiety that may come with making difficult decisions about finances.

We are in no position to tell individual borrowers whether advanced degrees are worth the cost. We emphasize that borrowers cannot focus just on earnings or just on cost to make informed decisions. Instead, students and policy makers should focus both on how much a person borrows for an advanced degree—as well as how much they can expect to earn—to consider whether that degree will pay for itself down the line.

Notes

1. "Salary Survey: Starting Salary Projections for Class of 2020 New College Graduates Data Reported by Employers; an Executive

Summary," National Association of Colleges and Employers, 2020. https://www.naceweb.org/uploadedfiles/files/2020/publication /executive-summary/2020-nace-salary-survey-winter-executive -summary.pdf.

2. Jaymes Pyne and Eric Grodsky, "Inequality and Opportunity in a Perfect Storm of Graduate Student Debt," *Sociology of Education* 93, no. 1 (September 20, 2019): 20–39. https://doi.org/10.1177/00380 40719876245.

Chapter 8

College Students Who Work More Hours Are Less Likely to Graduate

WALTER G. ECTON, *University of Michigan*

CAROLYN J. HEINRICH, *Vanderbilt University*

CELESTE K. CARRUTHERS, *University of Tennessee, Knoxville*

STUDENTS WHO WORK WHILE ENROLLED in college are about 20% less likely to complete their degrees than similar peers who don't work, which is a large and meaningful decrease in the predicted graduation rate. Among those who do graduate, working students take, on average, half a semester longer to finish. This is mainly because students who work many hours—over 15 hours a week—take fewer college credits per semester.

These findings come from our study published in 2023 in *AERA Open*,[1] a peer-reviewed open-access journal published by the American Education Research Association. To learn more about how work might affect a student's chances of graduation, we examined 17 years of data—2001 to 2017—from the state of Tennessee. We matched college student records to employment records for about 600,000 students. We compared working students with those who did not work but were otherwise similar in terms of family income, high school GPA, location, and demographic characteristics. We also looked at college progress for students who worked during some semesters, but not in others, to see whether they were more successful in completing their classes in semesters when they did not work.

Ultimately, we found that working students signed up for about one less credit on average per semester than did students who didn't work. This is likely because they had less time available for classes. Students who worked were every bit as successful in their classes after signing up, with similar course completion rates and similar GPAs. Still, because they signed up for fewer courses, their progression through college was slower, and they were less likely to graduate.

Notably, we did not see a decrease in graduation rates among students who worked less, especially less than eight hours per week. These students signed up for similar numbers of credits as their non-working classmates, and they completed their degrees at similar rates. This suggests that smaller amounts of work may not affect a student's progress toward graduation.

Why It Matters

Working while in college is very common, especially with the rising price of college tuition and the burden of student loan debt. Estimates for 2020 showed that 43% of full-time students and 81% of part-time students worked while enrolled in college.[2] In Tennessee, we found that working was especially common among community college students, first-generation students, and students returning to college as adults.

With so many students juggling work and school, colleges and policy makers could take more steps to support working students and help them meet their needs.[3] If working students take longer to complete college, policy makers could extend access to financial aid for longer periods if needed. For example, students can access federal Pell Grants for only 12 semesters. This may leave some students without an important source of financial aid if their employment causes them to take longer to finish their degree.

Students should be aware of the challenges that work might pose for their college journey. Work may be crucial for paying bills and creating opportunities for professional development. However, when students work 15 hours or more a week, they could have a harder time earning a college degree, which can ultimately enable a person to get a higher-paying job in the future.

What Still Isn't Known

One important question is whether certain jobs suit college students better than others. Some research suggests that on-campus jobs might be more convenient and help keep students focused on their classes. Students working in a job related to their major might find real-world connections between their job and classes—such as a nursing student working in a hospital. Given that work is a necessity for many students, educators can do more to guide students toward jobs that might increase their chance for college success.

Notes

1. Walter G. Ecton, Carolyn J. Heinrich, and Celeste K. Carruthers, "Earning to Learn: Working while Enrolled in Tennessee Colleges and Universities," *AERA Open* 9 (January 7, 2023). https://doi.org/10.1177/23328584221140410.
2. "College Student Employment," National Center for Education Statistics, last updated May 2022. https://nces.ed.gov/programs/coe/indicator/ssa/college-student-employment.
3. Lauren Remenick and Matt Bergman, "Support for Working Students: Considerations for Higher Education Institutions," *Journal of Continuing Higher Education* 69, no. 1 (September 2, 2020): 34–45. https://doi.org/10.1080/07377363.2020.1777381.

Part II.

Why College Still Matters

The financial argument for obtaining a college degree remains strong. On average, a graduate with a bachelor's degree outearns a graduate with a high school diploma. Additionally, the college graduate has better outcomes related to physical and mental health. In fact, they live longer—approximately 8.5 years longer on average. We already know that students who earn college degrees make more money, but we are also learning that they give back more in their communities.

The chapters in part II confront some of the core issues around both the individual and societal gains correlated with a college education. Neem addresses the need to look beyond the degree as merely documentation of workforce readiness. He makes the argument for college education for all Americans at all stages of life. These points are reinforced in Tampio's essay critiquing a focus on accountability solely related to postgraduate earnings. Like Neem, he sees the societal benefits of college-educated citizens in their overall contributions to communities both local and global. Other ways of articulating the value of a college education could focus on civic participation in voting, running for elected office, volunteering, and other forms of community engagement.

As Cuellar, Bencomo Garcia, and Saichaie point out, college graduates value giving back to society in a multitude of ways, and these differ based on college major. Unfortunately, the increasing expense of a college education has shifted the conversation about the value of college. The argument in favor of college has moved away from education's contributions to a more informed public and toward increased earning potential as students think about how they will repay loans after college, which influences their choice of major and decisions about the immediate economic return on investment.

When we consider the entire college payoff for students, it is much more than workforce readiness. It is important to take into consideration the impacts of both students' experiences and the knowledge they gained during their time in college. In addition, we need to look beyond the impacts of college on the lives of individual students and look to the impacts that those graduates will make on our collective future. In the face of rising challenges to democracy, disbelief in science, and climate change denial, we need a future with more educated citizens rather than a future with only an educated elite.

The current focus on social mobility as the only reason to attend college, a focus that is largely framed as a private benefit, is challenged by a generation of students who want to contribute to society in more than individual ways. Individuals can simultaneously strive both to make a family-sustaining wage and to contribute to society as an informed citizen.

Chapter 9

3 Things That Influence College Graduates from Rural Areas to Return to Their Communities

STEPHANIE SOWL, *ECMC Foundation*

WHEN HIGH-ACHIEVING STUDENTS from rural areas go off to college and graduate, they often choose to live in suburban or urban areas instead of rural communities like the one where they grew up, as decades of research have shown.[1] Often they are following the advice of adults—or just deciding on their own—to search for success in cities, where career opportunities are more abundant. Teachers, coaches, and neighbors might reinforce the message to leave behind the small-town life and its limited career opportunities.

That long-standing pattern might be changing, though.[2] Some rural communities are beginning to see their college graduates return.[3] I am a researcher who studies higher education and rural communities, and my colleagues and I wondered what might be leading adults to return to rural communities a decade or two after they graduate from college elsewhere.

We conducted a study using national data on the well-being of people, from their adolescence into adulthood, to look at why those who grew up in rural places decided to return.[4] Specifically, we considered whether their middle and high school experiences had any connection to their decision to return home in their late thirties or early forties. We included only those individuals who had gone at least 50 miles away to complete a bachelor's degree. We found three factors that contributed to college graduates coming back home.

1. Tight-Knit School Communities

We found that the more students enjoyed school in adolescence and felt as though they belonged, the more likely they were to move back to their rural hometown after leaving college. Even after considering demographic, neighborhood, and college characteristics, positive middle and high school experiences remained significant. This demonstrates the lasting value of supportive teacher-student and peer relationships.

This is consistent with other research finding that college graduates who returned had put down roots when growing up that made them feel grounded in their rural hometown. When students maintain relationships with people back home, it makes them feel as though they still belong when they return.[5]

Rural students who grow up with strong ties to their secondary schooling are more likely to return to their hometown after they graduate from college.
Education Images / Universal Images Group via Getty Images

2. Fewer People and More Land

College-educated people from smaller towns or open, undeveloped land were twice as likely to return home as people who grew up in slightly larger rural towns.

Rural places are rich with natural resources, from vast countrysides with fertile soil to dense forests that purify the air we breathe. Rural people are often attached to the natural environment,[6] and they have an appreciation for land.[7] Connecting with nature, breathing in fresh air, and enjoying peace and quiet can offer deep life satisfaction.[8]

3. Contributing to Their Communities

College graduates who grew up in rural communities where relatively few people went to college were more likely to return home than those from communities with more college-educated adults. Returners often feel a need to give back to their community. This has been accomplished by returners filling positions as doctors, lawyers, teachers, or entrepreneurs. They also volunteered to make a difference. College graduates provide several societal benefits, such as contributing to their community's economic growth, participating in community activities, and sharing new perspectives.[9]

A Focus on the Benefits

Our research comes at a time when some rural communities have begun to invest in local businesses, outdoor recreational activities, and local schools to attract both newcomers and returners.

Much attention has been given to a "rural brain drain," as described by sociologists Patrick J. Carr and Maria J. Kefalas, and to all the reasons why young people leave rural communities. But our research shows some of the characteristics of rural communities that have been associated with people returning home.

Notes

1. Robert M. Gibbs and John B. Cromartie, "Rural Youth Outmigration: How Big Is the Problem and for Whom?," *Rural America / Rural Development Perspectives* 10, no. 1 (1994): 9–16. https://doi.org /http://dx.doi.org/10.22004/ag.econ.311063.
2. Trevor Brooks, Sang-Lim Lee, Helen Berry, and Michael B. Toney, "The Effects of Occupational Aspirations and Other Factors on the Out-migration of Rural Youth," *Journal of Rural and Community*

Development 5, no. 3 (2010): 19–36. https://doi.org/https://journals
.brandonu.ca/jrcd/article/view/445/108.

3. Shaun A. Golding and Richelle L. Winkler, "Tracking Urbanization and Exurbs: Migration across the Rural–Urban Continuum, 1990–2016," *Population Research and Policy Review* 39, no. 5 (September 10, 2020): 835–59. https://doi.org/10.1007/s11113-020-09611-w.

4. Stephanie Sowl, Rachel A. Smith, and Michael G. Brown, "Rural College Graduates: Who Comes Home?," *Rural Sociology* 87, no. 1 (October 20, 2021): 303–29. https://doi.org/10.1111/ruso.12416.

5. Holly R. Barcus and Stanley D. Brunn, "Towards a Typology of Mobility and Place Attachment in Rural America," *Journal of Appalachian Studies* 15, nos. 1/2 (2009): 26–48. http://www.jstor.org/stable /41446817.

6. Jessica D. Ulrich-Schad, Megan Henly, and Thomas G. Safford, "The Role of Community Assessments, Place, and the Great Recession in the Migration Intentions of Rural Americans," *Rural Sociology* 78, no. 3 (July 9, 2013): 371–98. https://doi.org/10.1111/ruso.12016.

7. Diane K. McLaughlin, Carla M. Shoff, and Mary Ann Demi, "Influence of Perceptions of Current and Future Community on Residential Aspirations of Rural Youth," *Rural Sociology* 79, no. 4 (April 22, 2014): 453–77. https://doi.org/10.1111/ruso.12044.

8. John F. Helliwell, Hugh Shiplett, and Christopher P. Barrington-Leigh, "How Happy Are Your Neighbours? Variation in Life Satisfaction among 1200 Canadian Neighbourhoods and Communities," National Bureau of Economic Research working paper, May 2018. https://doi .org/10.3386/w24592.

9. Christiane von Reichert, John B. Cromartie, and Ryan O. Arthun, "Impacts of Return Migration on Rural U.S. Communities," *Rural Sociology* 79, no. 2 (October 3, 2013): 200–26. https://doi.org/10.1111 /ruso.12024.

Chapter 10

The Problem with the Push for More College Degrees

JOHANN N. NEEM, *Western Washington University*

IN A 2009 ADDRESS TO CONGRESS, President Barack Obama proclaimed that, by 2020, the United States would "once again have the highest proportion of college graduates in the world." A decade and a half later, it is worth asking how close we are to reaching that lofty goal and what have been the results of focusing so intently on college graduation rates as a sign of success.

In my work as a historian of education who wrote a book on the purpose of college,[1] I argue that a focus on degree attainment discounts the value of what a true college education provides. It places more emphasis on the piece of paper and less on the experience of college. This is harmful because it creates an impetus to expand the number of degrees without necessarily devoting resources to increasing access to college education.

State Support Declines

The number of Americans 25 years or older with a four-year college degree continues to rise, from 29.5% in 2009 to, according to a Lumina Foundation report, 37.3% in 2022.[2] However, despite the Obama administration's 2020 goal for college completion, state support for public colleges has fallen by about US$9 billion since then. In addition, large gaps in degree attainment remain between wealthy and poorer Americans and between racial and ethnic groups. Moreover, despite a steady increase in college degree attainment, the United States remains thirteenth in the world in the proportion of 25- to 34-year-olds who have earned a college degree.

In this context, elected leaders on both sides of the aisle, from Obama to former Wisconsin governor Scott Walker, called for new institutions and programs to provide fast, easy, and cheaper access to degrees, instead of the time, curricula, and professors that define a college education.

New Models Emerge

Responding to the call to speed students' progress toward degrees, two new nonprofit institutions, Western Governors University and Southern New Hampshire University's College for America, established online programs to award students credit for prior learning and meeting predetermined "competencies."

Simultaneously, public universities Arizona State University and Purdue University partnered with private corporations Pearson and Kaplan, respectively, to offer large numbers of online degrees without the kind of professorial oversight and interaction available to students on campus.

These approaches emphasize degree completion instead of the kinds of intellectual experiences that define a college education.

Elements of a College Education

In my book *What's the Point of College?*, I argue that what makes college distinct from other kinds of education is that a college education is not reducible to training. I also argue that a college education does not just certify competency but rather expands the mind in unpredictable ways. A college education requires time and interactions with professors and peers. And most of all, a college education requires opportunities to think without placing a value on the thought or seeking a specific outcome for it. Colleges should, ideally, encourage such reflection and insight.

I believe Obama's aspiration to increase the number of college graduates came at the cost of paying attention to the education that colleges should offer. The 2020 college completion goal shows that it is possible to increase the number of Americans with a college degree without necessarily increasing the number of Americans with a college education.

A Degree's Worth

Certainly, the United States should support good-faith efforts to increase job training for people with or without college degrees. Many of the fastest-growing jobs, in fields such as dental hygiene, health care support, and construction, require specialization but not a college education.

I worry, however, that a focus on economic outcomes could go too far. The Gates Foundation, for example, called for the evaluation of all college degrees based on their economic payoff. That is to say, the Gates Foundation wants to determine which degrees are a worthwhile investment. This would repeat the mistake of the Obama administration by again emphasizing the short-term salary gains of a college degree, rather than the broadening of the mind that comes with a college education. The emphasis that the Gates Foundation is placing on the economic value of a college degree threatens what makes college worthwhile—not just intellectually but also financially.

A college education is valuable in the labor market precisely because it cannot be reduced to one set of skills. What makes college graduates desirable is their ability to think broadly about the world and their capacity to use language and numbers well. These outcomes are achieved by having people spend a portion of their lives on campuses devoted to thinking as an end in itself.

I see a need for the United States to abandon its focus on degrees and instead support Americans—whether young or old, first-generation or legacy, poor or rich—to gain access to a true college education. This requires transforming America's colleges to make them available to people in all stages of life.

Older people—often with mortgages, children, or aging parents—need real and meaningful support to pursue a college education. If we Americans want more college-educated citizens, we must care about more than counting degrees.

Notes

1. Johann N. Neem, *What's the Point of College? Seeking Purpose in an Age of Reform* (Baltimore: Johns Hopkins University Press, 2019).
2. "A Stronger Nation," Lumina Foundation. https://www.lumina foundation.org/stronger-nation/report/#/progress.

Chapter 11

Beyond Social Mobility, College Students Value Giving Back to Society

MARCELA G. CUELLAR, *University of California, Davis*

ALICIA BENCOMO GARCIA, *Cabrillo College*

KEM SAICHAIE, *University of California, Davis*

STUDENTS WHO ARE THE FIRST IN THEIR FAMILY to attend college tend to see it as a means to improve their personal lives and as an opportunity for social mobility. That contrasts with the main message students get from policy makers and universities that largely emphasizes career growth.

This is the main finding from interviews we conducted with 21 undergraduate students at the University of California,

Davis, who were interested in education as a possible career.[1] Eleven of the students were first-generation college-goers. The rest were what we call continuing education students, that is, people whose parents went to college. They were all sophomores, juniors, or seniors. Our aim was to understand how first-generation students, defined as neither parent having attended college, view the role of higher education in their lives and in society.

Students tend to hear from parents, educators, and policy makers that a college degree should mainly be thought of as a ticket to a better career path. But in the interviews, we found that students weigh many goals when pursuing a college degree—ones that frequently shifted from social mobility to other, broader goals. These included professional development, learning for the sake of intellectual growth, pursuing careers with a purpose beyond earning potential, and contributing to society.

Most of the first-generation students we interviewed focused on social justice efforts like giving back to their communities and disrupting systemic inequities. For example, one student majoring in Chicana and Chicano studies and minoring in education said that even though teachers do not make a lot of money, her college education will allow her to help kids in low-income communities.

Students whose parents had attended college typically said that they see education as a way to help them become better citizens and critical thinkers.

Why It Matters

For over a century, scholars and policy makers have debated the purposes of college.

Increasingly, these conversations have emphasized social mobility, viewed as a private benefit, along with a combination of public goals, such as training workers and preparing citizens. Surveys show that more students are entering college to make more money, compared with the 1960s, when students sought a higher education for more holistic reasons, such as seeking a meaningful purpose in life.

Other scholars suggest that students have not fundamentally changed in what they expect. Rather, they say the way that colleges are funded has changed, with more of the cost falling on students and their families.

Our study, one of the few to ask students about this topic during their college attendance, confirms that some students still seek purpose above financial wealth. This finding runs counter to scholarly and popular discourse that focuses on neoliberal ideologies and postsecondary education as a means solely to enhance social mobility.

What Still Isn't Known

Our study may not reflect the views of students with other career interests or areas of study beyond education. Most of the first-generation students were Latina or Latino. The perspectives of first-generation peers from other racial backgrounds may differ.

What's more, we captured students' views at one point in time. Their thoughts about what they hope to gain from their college education may evolve, even after they graduate and enter the workforce.

Finally, this study was conducted prior to the pandemic. Findings may be different in a post–COVID-19 setting given the impact it had on historically marginalized students, many of whom are first-generation, and the increased attention paid to social justice issues.

What's Next

In future research, we plan to explore students' expectations about what a college education provides at different points in their studies. We also will consider how students' goals may differ by their major or the type of institution they attend. As more institutions seek better ways to support first-generation students, our understanding of what students expect and value from college, and how that may change through their years at college, should be further refined.

Note

1. Marcela G. Cuellar, Alicia Bencomo Garcia, and Kem Saichaie, "Reaffirming the Public Purposes of Higher Education: First-Generation and Continuing Generation Students' Perspectives," *Journal of Higher Education* 93, no. 2 (October 20, 2021): 273–96. https://doi.org/10.1080/00221546.2021.1979849.

Chapter 12

Gates-Funded Commission Aims to Put a Value on a College Education

NICHOLAS TAMPIO, *Fordham University*

THE GATES FOUNDATION is trying to disrupt American higher education with a Postsecondary Value Commission, which it launched in 2019. As its name suggests, the commission aims to define the value of a college degree. Among other things, the commission set out to "aid policymakers in gauging what the public gets for its investment in higher education."[1] If Congress listens to the commission, it could become harder for students majoring in the liberal arts or humanities to secure a federal loan or grant.

As a political scientist who researches education policy, I anticipate that the country will move to a two-tiered system. It will be one in which the affluent will be able to acquire a liberal arts education at elite private institutions, while students who depend on federal financial aid will be steered toward career-focused majors at public universities. In effect, the country will have one higher education system for the rich and another one for everyone else.

The Goals of the Commission

The Gates Foundation convened this commission to address a real problem: student debt. Total student loan debt in 2019 is US$1.77 trillion. There are nearly 44 million US borrowers with student loan debt. The commission is addressing a question that is on the minds of many families, policy makers, and taxpayers: Is college worth it?

The commission is defining college value to guide policy conversations. In a conference call with reporters in 2019, Mildred García, then commission co-chair and later chancellor of the California State University system, shared that she had just spent a day on Capitol Hill talking with legislators. She stated that "we are definitely hoping" that the commission's work will "affect" the reauthorization of the Higher Education Act that controls—among other things—how federal student aid is disbursed.

Just as the Gates Foundation pulled off a revolution in K–12 education with its support for the Common Core,[2] the foundation is serious about using policy advocacy and lobbying to enact "institutional transformation" of higher education.

For instance, commission member Anthony Carnevale, the director of Georgetown University's Center on Education and the Workforce, noted in 2019 how a move by then-president Donald Trump to focus more on outcomes of specific programs at colleges and universities is "one more step toward a widely supported movement to reorder higher education as we have known it." He continued: "In a shift toward program-level outcomes, every college will be unbundled down to the program level—its identity, traditions and structure will become less important."[3]

"Instead," Carnevale contended, "the outcomes of students in each particular major or field will be elevated in importance." Carnevale seemed to be aware of the potential threat this poses to the liberal arts. He remarked that society will have to "think of new models for assuring core liberal arts curricula that are essential to the well-rounded learning that students need."

Impact in Question

While the Gates commission aims to educate students and families about which colleges and majors are a worthwhile investment, this approach alone may not have much impact.

Presently the US Department of Education's College Scorecard collects and publicizes information about the debts and earnings of graduates from different colleges. Yet research has shown that most students do not respond to earnings data provided by the College Scorecard.[4] It's true that colleges with graduates who have higher median earnings have seen a slight rise in the SAT scores of students who enroll. The College Scorecard has also had some effect on where students from affluent public or private schools attend, but otherwise the College Scorecard does not influence who goes to college or where.[5]

Accountable to Whom?

So how can this commission transform American higher education when earlier reforms have not worked? It may be that it encourages Congress to make federal loans and grants available to students in some majors, such as engineering or business, where graduates tend to earn a high salary upon graduation. Conversely, Congress might be moved to make loans and grants unavailable for students in other majors, such as theology or a discipline of the humanities, where graduates do not earn as much.

Congress has already entertained this idea when it introduced the PROSPER Act. This higher education bill would have ended access to federal student loans for students enrolled in programs with low loan repayment rates. Democratic senators such as Elizabeth Warren of Massachusetts have co-sponsored the reintroduced College Transparency Act. The act would permit the federal government to collect earnings data on graduates from specific college programs and majors. Former Republican senator Lamar Alexander of Tennessee, past chairman of the Senate Education Committee, proposed rewriting the Higher Education Act to collect data on program-level outcomes.

Even former president Donald Trump joined the higher education accountability bandwagon, signing an executive order requiring the College Scorecard to publish program-level average earnings and loan repayment rates. In 2023, the Biden administration released regulations for establishing a framework of financial value transparency that collects and shares data about costs and expected financial outcomes of each college or career training program. According to

US Secretary of Education Miguel Cardona, "The Biden-Harris administration believes that when students invest in higher education, they should get a solid return on their investment."[6]

Where will this movement for higher education accountability lead?

According to Carnevale, it will lead to a "streamlining" of public university systems. Students at a flagship public university will still be able to major in English. But higher education must become accountable to stakeholders who don't want to subsidize "mediocre programs" on every branch campus.

Democracy and the Liberal Arts

Would it be a tragedy if society did not subsidize young people to major, if they so wish, in the liberal arts or humanities? Yes.

By focusing on the economic returns of higher education, the commission may lead policy makers to put less weight on the other reasons that students go to college, including to read humanity's greatest books, grapple with big questions about justice, study in other countries, work at internships, and think about what to do with the rest of one's life.

Notes

1. "Frequently Asked Questions," Postsecondary Value Commission, https://www.postsecondaryvalue.org/faq/.
2. Lyndsey Layton, "How Bill Gates Pulled Off the Swift Common Core Revolution," *Washington Post*, June 7, 2017. https://www.washington post.com/politics/how-bill-gates-pulled-off-the-swift-common-core -revolution/2014/06/07/a830e32e-ec34-11e3-9f5c-9075d5508f0a _story.html.

3. Anthony P. Carnevale, "The Revolution Is upon Us," *Inside Higher Ed*, March 25, 2019. https://www.insidehighered.com/views/2019/03/26/president-trumps-embrace-program-level-earnings-data-game-changing-opinion.
4. Adela Soliz, "Is College Choice Impacted by Data in the College Scorecard?," Brookings Institution, April 29, 2016. https://www.brookings.edu/blog/brown-center-chalkboard/2016/04/29/is-college-choice-impacted-by-data-in-the-college-scorecard/.
5. Michael Hurwitz and Jonathan Smith, "Student Responsiveness to Earnings Data in the College Scorecard," Social Science Research Network, revised September 29, 2017. https://doi.org/10.2139/ssrn.2768157.
6. "Biden–Harris Administration Announces Landmark Final Rules to Protect Consumers from Unaffordable Student Debt and Increase Transparency," press release, US Department of Education, September 27, 2023. https://www.ed.gov/news/press-releases/biden-harris-administration-announces-landmark-final-rules-protect-consumers-unaffordable-student-debt-and-increase-transparency.

Chapter 13

Fewer US College Students Are Studying a Foreign Language—and That Spells Trouble for National Security

DEBORAH COHN, *Indiana University Bloomington*

WHEN THE SOVIET UNION LAUNCHED *Sputnik 1,* the first artificial Earth satellite, on October 4, 1957, it did more than spark fears about America's ability to compete technologically. It also raised concerns that the United States had a shortage of Russian speakers capable of monitoring Soviet scientific and military activities. In 1958, the National Defense Education Act authorized funding to strengthen US education in language instruction, in addition to math and science.

More than six decades later, a 2023 Modern Language Association report raised concerns about America's foreign language capabilities anew. The report showed that the study of languages other than English at the university level experienced an unprecedented drop of 16.6% between 2016 and 2021.[1] The second-largest drop—of 12.6%—had taken place between 1970 and 1972. The recent decline continues a trend that began in 2009. Even though we live in an increasingly globalized world, the number of college students taking languages is rapidly falling.

As a professor of Spanish and Portuguese who researches trends in language education, I know that having fewer US college students who learn a foreign language increases risks for national security.

Foreign Language Census

Every few years since 1958, the Modern Language Association has conducted a census of enrollments in college-level language courses in the United States. The data shows that enrollments in languages other than English spiked following the passage of the National Defense Education Act.

Between 1958 and 1970, enrollments nearly tripled, from about 430,000 to almost 1.2 million. The bulk of students studied French, German, or Spanish. However, enrollments in Russian doubled in the first three years alone—jumping from roughly 16,000 in 1958 to over 32,700 in 1961. Enrollments in less commonly taught languages such as Chinese, Japanese, and Arabic also rose steeply.

After 1970, the enrollments in language study began to fall. Arabic was an exception. Although very few US students studied Arabic when the census began—just 364 in 1958,

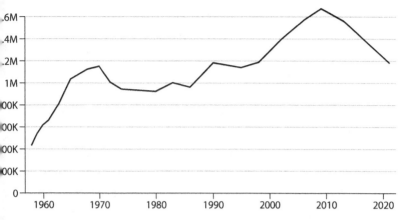

Enrollment in college courses for non-English languages over time. Number of students taking a foreign or Indigenous language class at a US college during the fall semester. K = thousand; M = million. *The Conversation, CC-BY-ND. Data from the Modern Language Association*

increasing to 1,324 in 1970—the 1973 oil crisis accelerated the trend, and enrollments passed 3,000 in 1977 before plateauing.

Role of Geopolitics

College enrollments in Russian and Arabic courses illustrate how language study can be directly affected by—and have implications for—political events.

Enrollments in Russian peaked at nearly 44,500 in 1990. The collapse of the Soviet Union in 1991 led to an immediate loss of interest in learning Russian. Enrollments dropped below 25,000 by 1995 and have continued to fall since. The latest survey of the Modern Language Association shows that, between 2016 and 2021 alone, enrollments fell from 20,353 to 17,598—just over 1,500 more than in 1958. The low number of US students learning Russian comes at a time of growing concerns over Russian military aggression in Europe, as well as Russia's role as a top cyber-threat, make knowledge of the language valuable to protecting national security.

Enrollments in Arabic, in turn, were low in 1998—just 5,505 college students studied the language. Training and hiring speakers with professional-level Arabic proficiency was not a priority for the federal government at that time.[2] As a result, the Federal Bureau of Investigation had few translators who were proficient in Arabic, which caused significant delays in translating surveillance information in the run-up to the September 11 attacks.

A year after 9/11, college-level enrollments in Arabic almost doubled to over 10,500, and they peaked in 2009 at just under 35,000.

Expansion Takes Time

Overcoming foreign language shortfalls is easier said than done. Gaps cannot be filled overnight, as languages viewed as critical to national security require hundreds to thousands of hours of study to reach professional proficiency. And it also takes time for universities to expand their language offerings and staffing.

Therefore, shortfalls have continued. In 2016, nearly a quarter of the State Department's overseas positions were held by people who did not meet the language proficiency requirement for their job. The numbers were even higher for positions requiring critical languages such as Arabic, Dari, Farsi, or Urdu. These language gaps have hindered officers' ability to protect embassies and manage emergency situations.

Steep Declines

After peaking in 2009 at almost 1.7 million, college-level enrollments in languages other than English fell steeply. The 2023 report of the Modern Language Association shows that, by 2021, enrollments had fallen to under 1.2 million—a drop of nearly 30%.

Enrollments in almost all of the most commonly taught languages dropped significantly during this window. Arabic fell by almost 35%, Mandarin by almost 25%, French by 37%, German by 44%, Japanese by 9%, and Spanish by 32%. The only exceptions to this decline were enrollments in American Sign Language, which increased 17%, and Korean, which increased 128%. Korean in particular stands out, as its enrollments have increased steadily since 1974 and have been boosted by a global fascination with Korean pop culture.

Overall, enrollments for 2021 were on par with those of 1998. And they were only slightly higher than those of 1970—even though more than twice as many students were attending college.

In addition to the Great Recession, other factors have contributed to the downturn in college language enrollments.[3] As of 2017, only about 20% of K–12 students study a foreign language, and only 11 states have foreign language requirements for high school graduation.

Meanwhile, according to the Pew Research Center, just 36% of Americans believe that knowing a foreign language is very important for workers to be successful.[4] In contrast, 85% believe that the ability to work with people from different backgrounds, training in writing and communication, and understanding how to use computers are each very important.

National Security Initiatives

In 2006, President George W. Bush launched the National Security Language Initiative to increase the number of speakers and teachers of critical languages.

Since then, government agencies have developed additional language programs. The National Security Agency's STARTALK, for example, organizes summer programs to teach critical languages to students in kindergarten through college and provides resources and opportunities for teachers. The program served almost 70,000 students and 15,000 teachers between 2007 and 2021. The National Security Language Initiative for Youth, in turn, is run by the State Department and offers summer and academic-year programs for high school students. Over 8,000 students have participated since 2006.

Despite the important role these programs play, the report of the Modern Language Association observed that college-level language enrollments have continued to decline, even at a time of growing need for knowledge of languages other than English in many industries. As history has shown us, these declines will likely have negative effects on national security, diplomacy, and US strategic interests.

Notes

1. *Enrollments in Languages Other than English in United States Institutions of Higher Education*, Modern Language Association, 2023. https://www.mla.org/Resources/Guidelines-and-Data/Reports-and-Professional-Guidelines/Enrollments-in-Languages-Other-Than-English-in-United-States-Institutions-of-Higher-Education.
2. Samuel G. Freedman, "After Sputnik, It Was Russian; After 9/11, Should It Be Arabic?," *New York Times*, June 16, 2004. https://www.nytimes.com/2004/06/16/nyregion/on-education-after-sputnik-it-was-russian-after-9-11-should-it-be-arabic.html.

3. Steven Johnson, "Colleges Lose a 'Stunning' 651 Foreign-Language Programs in 3 Years," *Chronicle of Higher Education*, January 22, 2019. https://www.chronicle.com/article/colleges-lose-a-stunning -651-foreign-language-programs-in-3-years.
4. "The State of American Jobs," Pew Research Center, October 6, 2016. https://www.pewresearch.org/social-trends/2016/10/06/the-state -of-american-jobs/.

Part III.

Education as a Private Good

In the United States, higher education is often framed as a private and individual good rather than as a public and societal good. The chapters in part III highlight some of the challenges that accompany this type of framing. The focus on career outcomes and earning potential reinforces this framing. Yet increased tax payments to the state and country are rarely linked with increased annual salaries, even though this is typically the case, as highlighted in the chapter by Simkovic. As earnings rise, so do the taxes that fund public goods. A college education increases the potential for a better job, better pay, a bigger house in a better neighborhood, and an increased ability to provide for loved ones. It also increases the potential for better health (and being less of a burden on society), better pay (thus increased taxes), more informed voters, more informed citizenry, and the ability to give back with time and treasure to local nonprofit organizations.

As a corollary to higher education being framed as a private good, colleges and universities are increasingly viewed as corporations and students as consumers. This is especially evident in the literature on mergers and closures, which overwhelming focuses on the financial health of an institution rather than on its public-serving mission. In the wake of increasing college closures, Lambert and Whittington recommend several ways to ascertain the financial health of a college when choosing where to attend. This leads students and their families to ask, "Will this institution exist 10 to 20 years from now?" rather than "Will this be the kind of institution that will help me become the person I aspire to be?" As Ott and Zimmerman point out, consumer protection has become a necessary part of policy discussions as enrollments increased in for-profit colleges, which have often been criticized for being too expensive and promoting high student loan debt.

With increased attention paid to the high cost of college attendance and rising student loan debt, many state and local governments are focused on finding ways to reduce the financial burden of a college education. Some of that is happening in public high schools through dual enrollment, early college, and year-13 programs, and most states are finding ways to provide tuition-free community college courses and to increase financial aid for students attending public four-year institutions. As the United States faces a historic low in its unemployment rate and the need for an increasingly educated workforce in a knowledge economy, leaders are discovering the downsides of having historically framed college education as a private good. If people are willing to do the work required to earn degrees, we should recognize the many ways in which this voluntary training benefits society as a whole and invest more in education, not just for the sake of individuals but for our collective future as well.

Chapter 14

Why Some Public Universities Get to Keep Their Donors Secret

ALEXA CAPELOTO, *John Jay College of Criminal Justice*

IN APRIL 2018, the public learned that George Mason University had let the Charles Koch Foundation have a say in the hiring and review of faculty. The revelation confirmed long-held suspicions that Virginia's largest public university was susceptible to pressure from wealthy donors to the university's foundation, which exists only to support the university.

The news raised questions as well. For example, how was the school able to conceal the strings-attached gift agreements for years? Do other public universities have similar arrangements, in which donations flow not to them

Texas A&M University (College Station)	$12.69 billion
University of Michigan (Ann Arbor)	$11.73 billion
University of Virginia (Charlottesville)	$6.86 billion
Ohio State University (Columbus)	$5.19 billion
University of Wisconsin (Madison)	$4.24 billion
University of Texas (Austin)	$4.04 billion
University of Washington (Seattle)	$3.53 billion
University of Minnesota (Twin Cities)	$3.5 billion
University of North Carolina (Chapel Hill)	$3.31 billion
Michigan State University (Lansing)	$3.31 billion

Ten biggest public-university endowments in the United States, ranging from US$3.3 billion to US$12.7 billion in assets, as of mid-2018. *The Conversation, CC-BY-ND. Data from the National Center for Education Statistics*

but to affiliated foundations? Most importantly, do these foundations give donors a legal right to shape a public institution of higher education without public oversight if they so choose?

As a journalist-turned-professor who researches the tension between privatization and the public's right to know, I can tell you that the vast majority of public colleges and universities have separate foundations that exist to receive and manage their private donations.[1] Unless state lawmakers do more to make the dealings of these foundations transparent, I'm concerned that there are few ways to detect the kind of influence allowed at George Mason.

George Mason Case

Transparent GMU, a student advocacy group formed in 2013, had tried for years to access the Koch agreements under

Virginia's Freedom of Information Act (VFOIA). The group suspected that George Mason might be trading academic influence for Koch dollars because of what the group had seen at other schools. For example, a strings-attached agreement forged in 2008 for a US$1.5 million donation from the Charles Koch Foundation to Florida State University caused a public outcry; Florida State later changed its policies.

Transparent GMU's VFOIA requests were denied on the basis that the George Mason University Foundation possessed the agreement records and, as a private entity, did not have to share them. The group sued the foundation in 2017. Transparent GMU argued that because the nonprofit accepts, disburses, and administers funds for the sole benefit of a public university, it should be subject to VFOIA requests just like the university.

More than a year later, while the case was still pending, the university released the agreements and acknowledged that allowing donors to influence decisions about faculty "falls short of the standard of academic independence we should expect in every gift." In the wake of the scandal, in May 2019, the university revised its gift acceptance policy. If the university agrees to any conditions attached to a donation, it must now acknowledge that agreement in writing, making the terms part of the public record and subject to VFOIA.[2] The Charles Koch Foundation also announced that it will now make public all multiyear agreements with colleges and universities.

But Transparent GMU ultimately lost its court challenge. In a unanimous decision that leaves no path for appeal, the Virginia Supreme Court ruled that as a privately held corporation with its own bylaws, the George Mason University

Foundation is not a public body. Therefore, it's not obligated to disclose records.

State by State

Unless the information is related to the federal government, public access to information is regulated state by state under a freedom of information law. Each state defines in its own way what constitutes a public body, public records, and public meetings.

Only Nevada explicitly defines university foundations as governmental entities under its public records act. A handful of other states, including Colorado, Georgia, and Minnesota, have laws dictating that foundations disclose certain financial records while still remaining private. In most cases, even in Nevada, donors' identities remain confidential.

Virginia's Freedom of Information Act applies to public agencies, bodies supported wholly or principally by public funds, and entities "of the public body created to perform delegated functions of the public body."

In its decision, the state's supreme court cited *Merriam-Webster's* dictionary definition of the word *of* in deciding that the George Mason Foundation wasn't a product "of" the university, even though it exists to support the school, pays the majority of the president's salary, operates on campus, is part of the GMU website and staff directory, and is considered a "component unit" in university accounting.

"Had the General Assembly intended the unreserved inclusion of nonprofit foundations, that exist for the primary purpose of supporting public institutions of higher education, as public bodies under VFOIA, it could have so provided, but it has not," Justice Cleo Powell wrote. "Policy determinations of this nature are peculiarly within the province of the General Assembly, not the judiciary."[3]

California Case

Courts in other states have followed the same logic. In 2001 a California appellate court found that the California State University, Fresno Association, a nonprofit that operates the university's commercial enterprises, wasn't a public agency under the California Public Records Act (CPRA).

The court looked at the language of the law, weighed it against the spirit of transparency, and saw a puzzling gap. "We are fully cognizant of the fact that our conclusion seems to be in direct conflict with the express purposes of the CPRA 'to safeguard the accountability of government to the public,'" Justice Rebecca Wiseman wrote. "The Legislature's decision to narrowly define the applicability of the CPRA, balanced against its sweeping goal to safeguard the public, leaves us scratching our judicial heads and asking, 'What was the Legislature thinking?'" Though the justice confessed to confoundment, courts don't act as super-legislatures to determine the wisdom or propriety of statutes: "The rewriting of a statute is a legislative, rather than a judicial function, a practice in which we will not engage."[4]

Ten years later, California passed a law that makes university foundations' financial records, contracts, and correspondence subject to public disclosure. Under the Richard McKee Transparency Act of 2011, donors can remain anonymous unless they receive something in exchange that's worth more than $2,500 or a no-bid contract within five years of the donation or unless they attempt to influence university curriculum or operations.

How Open Public Universities Need to Be about Fundraising

State laws are generally unclear about whether public-university foundations are subject to disclosure requirements. That leaves it up to the courts to decide what ought to happen, and so far the rulings have been mixed.

Following the George Mason court decision, David Bulova, a Democratic Virginia state delegate from Fairfax County, where the university's main campus is located, introduced two related bills preserving the private status of foundations that support public universities while also imposing new transparency requirements on them. Both passed and were signed into law in spring 2020.[5]

One makes the amount, date, purpose, and terms of a public-university donation subject to Virginia's Freedom of Information Act and only grants donor anonymity if the donor requests it and does not set conditions directing academic decision-making. The second follows George Mason University's lead, requiring that universities establish a process for reviewing, accepting, and documenting the terms and conditions of any donations that direct academic decision-making and for subjecting that documentation to VFOIA.

Both laws serve as good models for legislators in other states. Efforts to define university foundations as public entities usually go nowhere, but states can require more transparency of private organizations that are so clearly enmeshed with public institutions.

Notes

1. Alexa Capeloto, "A Case for Placing Public-University Foundations under the Existing Oversight Regime of Freedom of Information Laws," *Communication Law and Policy* 20, no. 4 (October 9, 2015): 311–42. https://doi.org/10.1080/10811680.2015.1078617.
2. "Gift Acceptance Policy," George Mason University policy no. 1123, sec. D, para. 1. https://universitypolicy.gmu.edu/policies/gift-acceptance-policy/.
3. Opinion by Justice Cleo E. Powell, in Transparent GMU v. George Mason University, Circuit Court of Fairfax County, December 12, 2019. https://www.vacourts.gov/opinions/opnscvwp/1181375.pdf.
4. California State University, Fresno Assn. v. Superior Court (McClatchy Co.), Ca. Fifth Dist. (July 16, 2001). Decision available from Justia Case Law, https://law.justia.com/cases/california/court-of-appeal/4th/90/810.html.
5. HB 1529, 2020 session of the General Assembly of Virginia, Virginia's Legislative Information System. https://lis.virginia.gov/cgi-bin/legp604.exe?201+sum+HB1529&201+sum+HB1529; HB 510 FOIA, 2020 session of the General Assembly of Virginia, Virginia's Legislative Information System. https://lis.virginia.gov/cgi-bin/legp604.exe?201+sum+HB510&201+sum+HB510.

Chapter 15

Free-College Proposals Should Include Private Colleges

MICHAEL SIMKOVIC, *University of Southern California*

STUDENTS CAN USE FEDERAL FINANCIAL AID to attend any college they want, whether public or private. But a number of "free college" proposals would increase federal funding only for community colleges or state-run universities. Private nonprofit universities would be excluded. The question is, Why?

From my vantage point as a scholar of the economics of higher education, I see a few factors at play.

A Question of Resources

One is cost. It would be easier to make higher education free to attend by covering only public institutions, which tend to charge lower tuition and to spend less educating each of their students. But cost and quality tend to go together, and this relationship holds true for higher education.

One way to measure quality is by tracking whether students complete their studies as planned. Four-year completion rates at public institutions trail those at private nonprofits by as much as 20% for students of the same race and sex. Colleges and universities with more funding and higher tuition—typically private institutions—not only graduate students faster, but their graduates also go on to earn higher salaries than their peers who graduate from less-well-funded colleges, after accounting for differences in student characteristics and selectivity. Several studies have come to similar conclusions,[1] namely, that educational resources affect graduates' earnings.[2]

Since students at public colleges graduate at lower rates and earn lower salaries, they tend to default on their student loans more often than those who went to private nonprofit colleges. Making federal money available to both public and private colleges could lead to fewer former students defaulting.

Quality and Spending

Ideally, federal funds provided by free-college initiatives would boost quality at colleges and universities. But covering tuition only at public institutions won't increase the quality of education at these schools unless it means the schools have more money to spend.

Poorer outcomes at public institutions can be explained by lower spending.[3] For example, during the 2020–21 school year, four-year public institutions spent about US$16,000 less than four-year private nonprofits per student per year. Two-year public colleges invest dramatically less.

But the resource problems at colleges won't get better if federal money merely pays the same tuition that students are paying now. Many state governments prohibit state colleges and universities from increasing tuition, even as states have cut the amount of money they spend per student. Tuition caps would prevent public colleges from obtaining the additional resources they need to improve quality. These price ceilings worsen problems such as high student-to-faculty ratios, low instructor pay, and restricted course offerings. They also mean that schools must turn away qualified students and allow facilities and equipment to fall into disrepair.

Without tuition caps, price would still be limited by market competition. Private nonprofits compete with one another for students and offer education across a range of prices and quality levels.

Some free-college proposals call for tying federal funding to state matching funds. But demanding more state funding could backfire. Some state governments might turn down federal funding for higher education if it requires that states spend more. The same thing happened when many states turned down Medicaid expansion.

Many students won't attend college unless it is close to home or is in a city where they hope to settle. Restricting these students to public institutions would limit their choice of academic programs and quality. For example, in some parts of the country, only private institutions offer programs like business economics or electromechanical engineering. Including private institutions would mean a wider range of choices.

How It Could Work

What could a federal subsidy look like that would empower students to choose the college they believe is best for them?

One option would be a voucher that would fund costs at a school of the student's choice. For instance, a voucher could cover between 30% and 80% of tuition, fees, books, and reasonable living expenses at any accredited public or private nonprofit college or university. Investing more public dollars in higher education would boost income and employment, which would lead to more tax revenue and thus would benefit the general public.[4]

Some proposals have called for means-tested public funding for higher education. Means-tested funds are only made available to those who can prove they fall below a certain income or wealth threshold. Yet public investments in education do not have to be limited to the poor to help the poor. Programs that only benefit the poor are more prone to budget cuts than more universal programs.

Including private nonprofit institutions in affordability programs—or free-college proposals—will benefit middle-income and poor students. Many private nonprofit institutions seek to include and assist qualified students from less privileged backgrounds.[5] Indeed, some of the most selective institutions—and typically the best funded—have been among the most generous with respect to assisting students with financial need.[6] With more government support, private institutions could more easily educate more of these students.

Some might argue that making education funding available to private institutions would divert funding from public universities. On the flip side, respecting student choice might make a funding program more popular and build broader political support for increased funding for higher education.

Notes

1. Dominic J. Brewer, Eric R. Eide, and Ronald G. Ehrenberg, "Does It Pay to Attend an Elite Private College? Cross-Cohort Evidence on the Effects of College Type on Earnings," *Journal of Human Resources* 34, no. 1 (Winter 1999): 104–23. https://doi.org/10.2307/146304; Dan A. Black and Jeffrey A. Smith, "How Robust Is the Evidence on the Effects of College Quality? Evidence from Matching," *Journal of Econometrics* 121, nos. 1–2 (2004): 99–124. https://doi.org/10.1016/j.jeconom.2003.10.006.

2. Dan A. Black and Jeffrey A. Smith, "Estimating the Returns to College Quality with Multiple Proxies for Quality," *Journal of Labor Economics* 24, no. 3 (July 2006): 701–28. https://doi.org/10.1086/505067.

3. Marc Scott, Thomas Bailey, and Greg Kienzl, "Relative Success? Determinants of College Graduation Rates in Public and Private Colleges in the U.S.," *Research in Higher Education* 47, no. 3 (May 2006): 249–79. https://doi.org/10.1007/s11162-005-9388-y.

4. Michael Simkovic, "The Knowledge Tax," *University of Chicago Law Review* 82 (2015): 1981–2043. https://heinonline.org/HOL/Page?handle=hein.journals/uclr82&id=2005&collection=journals&index=.

5. Caroline M. Hoxby and Christopher Avery, "The Missing 'One-Offs': The Hidden Supply of High-Achieving, Low Income Students," National Bureau of Economic Research working paper, December 2012. https://doi.org/10.3386/w18586.

6. Caroline M. Hoxby and Sarah Turner, "What High-Achieving Low-Income Students Know about College," *American Economic Review* 105, no. 5 (2015): 514–17. https://www.aeaweb.org/articles?id=10.1257/aer.p20151027.

Chapter 16

5 Ways to Check a College's Financial Health

LEO M. LAMBERT, *Elon University*

GERALD WHITTINGTON, *Elon University*

THE FINANCIAL HEALTH OF COLLEGES and universities is much in the news these days. An enrollment cliff—a drop-off in traditionally aged college students—will hit in this decade and may threaten small, regional, and marginally resourced colleges and universities. An article in *Forbes* offered some sound advice: "If you are worried or even curious about the financial health of a college, ask them. It's a good, reasonable question for any student, parent or community leader to ask."[1]

But what are the right questions to ask? As longtime university administrators with experience at both public and private institutions, we suggest some questions to ask and research to do.

1. What Physical Shape Is the School In?

Institutions with cash-flow problems often put off millions of dollars of maintenance—and it shows. As you tour a campus, you will probably form an impression in a short time of what the campus is like. Is it clean and neat? Is there evidence of disrepair? Do the buildings appear well cared for and technologically up-to-date? All these things shine light on whether an institution has the resources needed to keep its facilities in good operating order. The more you see that concerns you, the more you should wonder if a school has enough money to provide a quality educational experience.

2. How Big Is Its Endowment?

When it comes to a college or university's endowment, size matters. An endowment is a permanent fund that universities and their foundations use to collect and invest funds given by philanthropic donors. Most schools use interest and dividends earned from the funds in their endowment to pay for various things, such as student aid programs and financial support for study abroad and internships.

You can find out how large an institution's endowment is through an online search. Generally speaking, the larger the endowment, the better able an institution is to finance its operations and the more stable it is for the long run. Only 132 institutions have endowments of more than US$1 billion.[2] But the size of the endowment isn't the only thing to consider.

To preserve the value of endowment spending for both current and future students, colleges were customarily advised to spend only about 5% of their endowment each year. Institutions that spend above that amount over a longer period of time can potentially erode the value of their endowment, unless they attract more donations or gain other sources of revenue.

For that reason, institutions that spend more than 5% assume a larger risk for the future market value of the endowment. An endowment spending rate of more than 5% may also be a sign of budgetary stress. There is no single place that you can go to find out the spending rate for an endowment. Some institutions, such as Elon University, where we both work, and Yale University, publish this information on their websites. Many do not.

Often, the only way to find out is to ask. You might start by asking the director of admissions or the chief financial officer.

3. What Is the Tuition Discount Rate?

At private colleges, you should ask, "What is the school's tuition discount rate?" This discount is tuition dollars that families or students pay that are redistributed—for good reason—to support students with financial need or to attract students with special talents. Learning environments that are diverse and vibrant benefit all students.[3] This tuition money gets redistributed in the form of need-based financial awards, merit financial awards, and athletic financial awards.

According to the National Association of College and University Business Officers, the average tuition discount rate for incoming freshmen in 2018–19 was 56.2%.[4] When an institution is using 56% of every dollar they take in for discounting, that leaves only 44% for everything else, such as faculty and staff salaries, student support services, and facilities and utilities. A tuition discount rate higher than the average rate can be a sign of trouble.

If you have never understood why the sticker price of college is not what you end up paying, a big part of that answer for private colleges is the tuition discount rate.

4. Check Databases

Check out federal databases to get key measures about a school's performance. The College Scorecard, for instance, is a free website of the US Department of Education that provides information on a variety of measures, including the size of the student body, cost, graduation rates, and how much students are expected to earn after they graduate.

The Department of Education also publishes something called a "financial responsibility composite score" for each institution in the country that receives federal aid. This score rates each school's ability to meet the standards of financial responsibility necessary to participate in federal financial aid programs. Scores range from a high of 3 to a low of –1. While this one score doesn't tell the full fiscal story of a school, it is a key indicator of whether the school is in good financial health.

5. Search Online

Many state university systems are considering school mergers because of declining enrollment. Researching online the institutions you are considering will help you uncover potential trouble spots: Is the school's accreditation threatened? Has enrollment been on the decline? Has there been frequent turnover in leadership? If the answer is yes, none of these things bodes well for a college or university in the future.

There are more than 4,500 colleges and universities in the United States. Most of them can make a major positive difference in a student's life. But some are in danger of closing and—in the most egregious cases—are revolving doors of failure. Before you invest your money by paying tuition to attend a school, or by footing the bill for a loved one to go, understand that the responsibility for doing research and asking questions is on you.

Notes

1. Derek Newton, "We Don't Need a List of College Finances," *Forbes*, November 22, 2019. https://www.forbes.com/sites/dereknewton /2019/11/22/we-dont-need-a-list-of-college-finances/?sh=238d 91168995.
2. Josh Moody, "College Endowment Returns Fall after Soaring High." *Inside Higher Ed*, February 16, 2023. https://www.insidehighered.com /news/2023/02/17/college-endowments-dropped-fiscal-year-2022.
3. Anthony Lising Antonio, Mitchell J. Chang, Kenji Hakuta, David A. Kenny, Shana Levin, and Jeffrey F. Milem, "Effects of Racial Diversity on Complex Thinking in College Students," *Psychological Science* 15, no. 8 (August 2004): 507–10. https://doi.org/10.1111/j.0956-7976 .2004.00710.x.
4. Josh Moody, "Tuition Discount Rates Hit New High," *Inside Higher Ed*, April 25, 2023. https://www.insidehighered.com/news/business /revenue-strategies/2023/04/25/tuition-discount-rates-hit-new -high.

Chapter 17

Cost and Lack of Majors Are among the Top Reasons Why Students Leave For-profit Colleges

MOLLY OTT, *Arizona State University*

THOMAS ZIMMERMAN, *Rutgers University*

FOR THE MAJORITY OF STUDENTS, the college where they enroll is often the one from which they will graduate. Not so for the approximately one million students who transfer each year from one school to another. Of these one million, about 100,000 students transfer from one of the approximately 2,300 for-profit universities that exist in the United States. That's a sizable portion of the roughly 777,000 students who attend for-profit colleges.

As researchers of higher education, we are interested in why students leave for-profit universities. These schools have been criticized for deceptive recruiting practices, for being overpriced,[1] and for failing to adequately prepare graduates for well-paying jobs.[2] In an effort to better understand the reasons behind the transfers, we interviewed 12 students who had transferred from a private for-profit to a public nonprofit university in the fall of 2021. Below are four main themes that emerged from our interviews.[3]

1. Too Expensive

Affordability came up repeatedly among the students we interviewed. A quarter said attending a for-profit initially seemed less expensive than a public university option. After they enrolled, however, costs went up. They received a scholarship from the for-profit but did not realize it covered the first year only and was not renewable. Their experiences are not unusual. Financial aid offers are often vague about the total costs that students are expected to pay.

Half of those we interviewed also shared that they had to take out loans to cover the balance, despite having received institutional scholarships. As they watched their debt grow, particularly when initial scholarships had expired, they realized that transferring to a public university would be cheaper.

Their experiences are consistent with national trends that show college students who attend for-profits are more likely to have student loan debt—with higher balances—than students enrolled at other types of schools. A 2019 study found that 74% of full-time students who attended for-profit colleges had outstanding loans, compared with 21% at community college and 47% at four-year public schools. On an annual basis, for-profit students borrowed about US$8,000, compared with the average community college student's debt of approximately US$4,700 and four-year public college student's average of US$7,000.[4]

As of the 2020–21 academic year, the average net cost of attendance at for-profit institutions was US$24,600 and was US$14,700 at public institutions.

2. Lack of Majors

About half of those we interviewed transferred in part because their original school did not offer their desired major. Some initially chose the for-profit for reasons like convenient location, an easy admission process, or perceived affordability. Later they realized that none of the majors offered were exactly what they wanted. For others, their interests had shifted over time.

For-profit universities mainly offer majors that are vocationally oriented and do not cost much to teach, such as business, engineering-related technologies, and health professions. Nonprofit institutions tend to have more diverse offerings.

We found that, before they decided to transfer, most students had asked their academic adviser to help them identify alternative majors. Though this may seem like a good idea, the reality is that many for-profit universities, in an effort to keep revenue flowing, often direct their employees to find ways to keep students enrolled.

Indeed, several students told us their adviser had recommended staying and switching to a different major rather than exploring options at other schools that may better align with their interest. The adviser for one aspiring lawyer initially suggested the for-profit's justice studies major. After taking introductory courses, the student realized that justice studies was intended for future law enforcement officers, not lawyers. The adviser then placed her in the university's government program, which was also not a good fit.

The student independently researched the best majors for future lawyers and determined that political science would be the best preparation. Since the for-profit university did not have a political science program, she transferred to a public university.

3. Inflexible Schedules

Unlike students at nonprofit and public universities, students at for-profit universities don't get to pick the classes they take. Students are enrolled in courses each term by their academic adviser without much choice over the course's topical focus, the professor who'll teach it, or the day and time the class is taught.

The predetermined structure of for-profit degree programs appeals to some students, such as those with caretaking responsibilities or inflexible work schedules. We found, however, that the practice also motivated many to transfer. While they valued advisers' input, the students we interviewed wanted more transparency, control, and freedom over their schedules and choices of instructors and course topics.

4. Questions of Quality

Scholars and policy makers have long called the quality of for-profit colleges into question. Only two students we interviewed mentioned quality as a reason for transferring. They had concerns that instructors were inexperienced and courses were too easy.

The Biden administration recently proposed new rules, referred to as gainful employment regulations, aimed at ensuring degrees lead to positive employment outcomes for graduates. The rules would revoke the ability of schools to offer students federal financial aid if graduates' student loan payments exceed 8% of their income or 20% of their discretionary income. The US Department of Education states that the objective is to "ensure quality and accountability in postsecondary education."

Here's What Students Can Do

To avoid the potential pitfalls associated with for-profit colleges, we suggest a few options that students can explore prior to enrollment.

They may want to pay attention to academic program structure, costs, and quality. Seeking information from sources unaffiliated with any specific university is a good strategy. The Bureau of Labor Statistics' online Occupational Outlook Handbook has good information about majors that lead to different jobs. Schools that do not offer majors that lead to a student's desired career should be avoided.

The College Scorecard, an online tool provided by the US Department of Education, lets people search for schools according to majors offered, location, and other criteria. With search filters set, the College Scorecard provides earnings and student debt data for recent graduates.

Students should also pay close attention to the fine print of financial aid packages. In particular, students should find out whether a scholarship offer is renewable. If the answer is yes, it pays to know what criteria the recipient must met to maintain eligibility for the scholarship. If a scholarship is not renewable, students should account for this when estimating the overall cost of attending the school over the expected span of time it takes to earn a degree.

Our research shows that for-profit institutions may be less affordable in the long run than they initially appear. Conversely, nonprofit institutions that initially seem more expensive than for-profit institutions may be more affordable over the course of a student's progress toward a degree.

Notes

1. Stephanie Riegg Cellini, "For-profit Higher Education: An Assessment of Costs and Benefits," *National Tax Journal* 65, no. 1 (March 1, 2012): 153–79. https://doi.org/10.17310/ntj.2012.1.06.
2. Stephanie Riegg Cellini, "For-profit Colleges in the United States: Insights from Two Decades of Research," EdWorkingPaper, May 2021. https://doi.org/10.4324/9780429202520-18.
3. Molly Ott and Thomas Zimmerman, "Exploring Between-Sector Transfers: Why For-profit University Students Switch to Public Institutions," *Journal of College Student Retention*, March 12, 2023. https://doi.org/10.1177/15210251231161828.
4. Cellini, "For-profit Colleges in the United States."

Part IV.

Inequality and the Failure of Social Systems

The chapters in part IV focus on the attempts that higher education has made to mitigate the failures of our country's social support systems, which surface in dramatic ways on our college campuses. These supports include necessities such as childcare for student parents, reliable Wi-Fi, and food assistance for those who are food insecure. Although the provision of a social safety net for college students should not be the responsibility of higher education, increasingly this has become the case. These systemic issues are a failure of our society to provide for those who are trying to improve their lives through education, and colleges and universities are working to make up for these systemic failures.

The education of college students is an investment in the future workforce and the future of our democracy. It is unconscionable to ignore the food and housing insecurity of our students. Over 35% of college students currently experience food insecurity, and as Martinez points out, food-insecure students struggle to maintain their mental and physical well-being and ultimately pay the price with lower academic success.

Kuperberg and Mazelis highlight that not only are poor students skipping meals, but they are also skipping health care and medicine. Food and health care are basic needs and should also be basic rights. It defies logic as to why we would starve the development of the minds that represent our best hope for a better future.

In addition to food pantries, Wi-Fi hotspots, and transportation vouchers, prison education programs are another way that colleges and universities are attempting to repair the damages of societal failures and to build a better future for all of us. Gellman highlights the work of her college's prison initiative and the "transformational power of education" to change lives through adult basic education, English-language instruction, and college degrees.

In a world where basic needs were met, colleges and universities wouldn't have to make up for these equity gaps. As lots of us discovered during the pandemic, though, for many of our students, campus is their only home, and its cafeterias are their primary source of food.

Chapter 18

College Students with Loans More Likely to Report Bad Health and Skip Medicine and Care

ARIELLE KUPERBERG, *University of Maryland, Baltimore County*

JOAN MAYA MAZELIS, *Rutgers University–Camden*

STUDENTS WHO TOOK OUT LOANS TO PAY for college rated their physical health and mental health as being worse than those who didn't take out student loans. They also reported more major medical problems and were more likely to report delaying medical, dental, and mental health care and using less medication than the amount prescribed to save money.

We reported these findings in an article published in the *Journal of American College Health*.[1] The findings are based on surveys collected in 2017 from over 3,200 college students attending two public universities in the United States.

We asked students to rate their physical and mental health on a four-point scale—excellent, good, fair, and poor. We also asked if they had experienced any major medical problems in the past year or whether they had ever postponed medical, dental, or mental health care to make ends meet since starting college. Those who indicated they were regularly taking medication for physical health problems, such as asthma or high blood pressure, were asked if they ever took less medication than prescribed to save money.

Students with loans reported worse outcomes than those without loans, even after accounting for differences between them in terms of race, age, and gender as well as their parents' education level and marital status.

Despite their worse self-reported mental health, students with loans were equally likely as students without loans to have received a new mental health diagnosis or treatment for a mental disorder in college. They also were equally likely to have visited a mental health practitioner in the past year or to use mental health medication. But they were almost twice as likely as those without debt to report delaying mental health care.

Why It Matters

Our findings suggest that student loans may have hidden costs in the form of worse physical and mental health, more medical problems, and diminished use of medical and mental health care. Stress from student loans can affect students while they are still in college,[2] harming both mental and physical health.[3]

Students are often at a crucial juncture when they enter college,[4] a time when they are first leaving their parents' home and establishing habits—such as those related to medical and dental care—that may persist beyond college.[5] Declining to seek medical care can result in worse medical problems,[6] potentially leading to diminished health and shorter lives for college graduates with loans.[7]

One of the advantages of getting a college degree is improved health.[8] Students who take out loans to attend college, however, may not see those benefits, especially if they defer medical care or use less medicine to save money.

Previous generations had greater access to free or low-cost public higher education.[9] This access eroded as state budgets failed to keep up with the rising demand for and costs of higher education.[10] The current system of higher education funding requires most people to take on debt to get a college degree; recent national data indicates that among 2019 graduates of public or private nonprofit four-year universities, 62% had student debt.[11]

What's Next

We are writing a book that explores how debt affects life after college, including the consequences for health, housing, romantic relationships, and career trajectories. So far, we have found that inequalities in health and delays in doctor visits persist after graduation. College graduates who put off doctor visits to save money while in college were a little over twice as likely to experience a recent major medical problem 15 months and 3.5 years after graduation. We also found they were over four times as likely to be putting off medical care to save money after graduation, showing these habits persist well after they leave college.

Notes

1. Arielle Kuperberg, Kenneshia Williams, and Joan Maya Mazelis, "Student Loans, Physical and Mental Health, and Health Care Use and Delay in College," *Journal of American College Health*, January 3, 2023. https://doi.org/10.1080/07448481.2022.2151840.

2. Sonya L. Britt, David Allen Ammerman, Sarah F. Barrett, and Scott Jones, "Student Loans, Financial Stress, and College Student Retention," *Journal of Student Financial Aid* 47, no. 1 (April 3, 2017). https://doi.org/10.55504/0884-9153.1605.

3. Alisia G. Tran, Jeffrey S. Mintert, Jasmín D. Llamas, and Christina K. Lam, "At What Costs? Student Loan Debt, Debt Stress, and Racially/Ethnically Diverse College Students' Perceived Health," *Cultural Diversity and Ethnic Minority Psychology* 24, no. 4 (October 2018): 459–69. https://doi.org/10.1037/cdp0000207.

4. Jennifer Lynn Tanner, "Recentering during Emerging Adulthood: A Critical Turning Point in Life Span Human Development," in *Emerging Adults in America: Coming of Age in the 21st Century*, ed. Jeffrey Jensen Arnett and Jennifer Lynn Tanner (Washington, DC: American Psychological Association, 2006), 21–55. https://doi.org/10.1037/11381-002.

5. Melissa C. Nelson, Mary Story, Nicole I. Larson, Dianne Neumark-Sztainer, and Leslie A. Lytle, "Emerging Adulthood and College-Aged Youth: An Overlooked Age for Weight-Related Behavior Change," *Obesity: A Research Journal* 16, no. 10 (September 6, 2012): 2205–11. https://doi.org/10.1038/oby.2008.365.

6. Alexander Thomas, Javier Valero-Elizondo, Rohan Khera, Haider J. Warraich, Samuel W. Reinhardt, Hyeon-Ju Ali, Khurram Nasir, and Nihar R. Desai, "Forgone Medical Care Associated with Increased Health Care Costs among the U.S. Heart Failure Population," *JACC: Heart Failure* 9, no. 10 (October 2021): 710–19. https://doi.org/10.1016/j.jchf.2021.05.010.

7. Joel S. Weissman, Robert Stern, Stephen L. Fielding, and Arnold M. Epstein, "Delayed Access to Health Care: Risk Factors, Reasons, and Consequences," *Annals of Internal Medicine* 114, no. 4 (February 15, 1991): 325–31. https://doi.org/10.7326/0003-4819-114-4-325.

8. Katrina M. Walsemann, Bethany A. Bell, and Robert A. Hummer, "Effects of Timing and Level of Degree Attained on Depressive Symptoms and Self-Rated Health at Midlife," *American Journal of*

Public Health 102, no. 3 (March 1, 2012): 557–63. https://doi.org/10.2105/ajph.2011.300216.

9. John R. Thelin, *A History of American Higher Education*, 3rd ed. (Baltimore: Johns Hopkins University Press, 2019).

10. Michael Hout, "American Higher Ed Isn't Doing the Job," *Contexts* 8, no. 1 (February 2009): 76–76. https://doi.org/10.1525/ctx.2009.8.1.76; Robert B. Archibald and David H. Feldman, *The Anatomy of College Tuition*, American Council on Education. https://www.acenet.edu/Documents/Anatomy-of-College-Tuition.pdf.

11. Melanie Hanson, "Student Loan Debt Statistics," Education Data Initiative, updated March 3, 2024. https://educationdata.org/student-loan-debt-statistics; *Student Debt and the Class of 2019*, fifteenth annual report, Institute for College Access & Success, October 2020. https://ticas.org/wp-content/uploads/2020/10/classof2019.pdf.

Chapter 19

3 Things the COVID-19 Pandemic Taught Us about Inequality in College—and Why They Matter Today

ELENA G. VAN STEE, *University of Pennsylvania*

ELISE, A NURSING STUDENT at an elite US university in the Northeast, found herself back home and sleeping on the floor of her parents' one-bedroom apartment after the COVID-19 pandemic was declared in March 2020.

It was tough to get a good night's sleep as family members passed through to the kitchen or the front door. Such interruptions also made it difficult to concentrate during virtual lectures and exams. Sometimes, limited internet bandwidth made it impossible for Elise to attend class at all. She couldn't ask her parents to buy her a new computer to replace the one that was breaking down, she explained, because she knew they couldn't afford it.

Meanwhile, Elise's classmate, Bella, a business student and the daughter of two Ivy League–educated professionals, had two empty bedrooms at her parents' home. She used one for sleep, the other for schoolwork. Her parents had purchased "a monitor and all these other accessories to help make studying easier."

As a doctoral candidate in sociology, I study inequality among young adults. Elise and Bella are 2 of the 48 undergraduates I interviewed to understand how college students from different socioeconomic backgrounds dealt with COVID-19 campus closures.[1] Although all attended the same elite university, upper-middle class students like Bella often enjoyed academic and financial benefits from parents that their less affluent peers like Elise did not.

Just because most college students have gone back to in-person classes doesn't mean these disparities have gone away.[2] Here are three lessons from the pandemic that can help colleges better address student inequality going forward.[3]

1. The Digital Divide Disrupts Learning

Elise wasn't the only student in my study who didn't have the learning technology she needed. "It was a solid two and a half weeks where I didn't have a laptop," said Shelton, a social sciences major, describing how he wrote a four-page research paper on his phone. Although Shelton had secured a laptop by the time I interviewed him in June 2020, he still didn't have Wi-Fi in his off-campus apartment.

Before the pandemic, college students could typically use their school's computer labs and internet hot spots on campus. During remote instruction, however, many had to join classes from smartphones or park outside stores to access free Wi-Fi. Although most undergraduates own a cell phone and laptop, the functionality of these devices and their ability to stay connected to the internet are not equal.[4]

2. Living Conditions Are Learning Conditions

When residential universities sent undergraduates home in March 2020, some students did not have a home they could safely return to. Others, including some in my study, feared exposing parents to COVID-19 or being a financial burden. Still others had concerns about space, privacy, internet access, or disruptions from family members.

"I didn't even have a desk at home," recalled Jennifer, a major in a STEM discipline (science, technology, engineering, and mathematics), who stayed in a friend's living room before moving to her grandparents' house.

Even before the pandemic, students living in dormitories were in the minority. Far more undergraduates live off campus, many with their parents. In a fall 2019 survey, 35% of four-year college students and half of community college students reported housing challenges, which included being unable to pay rent and leaving a household because they felt unsafe.

The struggles of students like Jennifer call attention to socioeconomic divides for students who were living off campus all along. These include inequalities in space, quiet, and furniture for studying.

3. Many Students Are Family Caregivers, Too

Finally, the pandemic increased many students' caregiving responsibilities, which sometimes limited the time they could spend on schoolwork.[5]

For example, Ashley, a social sciences major, described how she shopped, cooked, and managed her younger siblings' remote schooling while her mom worked a retail job. "It wasn't necessarily a bad thing that I was [home] to help, but it definitely impaired my studies," she told me. Before the pandemic, Ashley had helped support her family financially from a distance. But her responsibilities grew when she returned home and was the only adult available to help her younger siblings.

Contrary to the popular idea of college as a time of self-focused exploration, recent studies describe ways that some students—often from low-income, minority, or immigrant families—support their families.[6] These include sending money home, helping siblings with homework, assisting parents with digital technology,[7] and chaperoning medical appointments. Such responsibilities are often invisible to university instructors and administrators. Students are members of families and communities, and they enter the classroom with different resources and responsibilities. Inclusive classrooms require instructors to demonstrate awareness, empathy, and flexibility around these differences.

But empathy won't fix students' laptops or pay their rent. The pandemic highlighted inequalities that are reinforced by universities designed for so-called traditional college students—fresh out of high school, living on campus, financially supported by their parents, and having few caregiving responsibilities. Yet such students are a privileged minority.

Notes

1. Elena G. van Stee, "Privileged Dependence, Precarious Autonomy: Parent / Young Adult Relationships through the Lens of COVID-19," *Journal of Marriage and Family* 85, no. 1 (November 16, 2022): 215–32. https://doi.org/10.1111/jomf.12895.
2. Alanna Gillis and Laura M. Krull, "COVID-19 Remote Learning Transition in Spring 2020: Class Structures, Student Perceptions, and Inequality in College Courses," *Teaching Sociology* 48, no. 4 (September 22, 2020): 283–99. https://doi.org/10.1177/009205 5x20954263.
3. Elena G. van Stee, "Parenting Young Adults across Social Class: A Review and Synthesis," *Sociology Compass* 16, no. 9 (August 11, 2022). https://doi.org/10.1111/soc4.13021.
4. Amy L. Gonzales, Jessica McCrory Calarco, and Teresa Lynch, "Technology Problems and Student Achievement Gaps: A Validation and Extension of the Technology Maintenance Construct," *Communication Research* 47, no. 5 (August 31, 2018): 750–70. https://doi.org /10.1177/0093650218796366.
5. Krista M. Soria, Molly McAndrew, Bonnie Horgos, Igor Chirikov, and Daniel Jones-White, "Undergraduate Student Caregivers' Experiences during the COVID-19 Pandemic: Financial Hardships, Food and Housing Insecurity, Mental Health, and Academic Obstacles." Center for Studies in Higher Education, University of California, Berkeley, September 17, 2020. https://escholarship.org/uc/item/7h06q880.
6. Blair Harrington, "'It's More Us Helping Them Instead of Them Helping Us': How Class Disadvantage Motivates Asian American College Students to Help Their Parents," *Journal of Family Issues* 44, no. 7 (January 3, 2022): 1773–95. https://doi.org/10.1177/0192513x2 11064867.
7. Rebecca Covarrubias, Ibette Valle, Giselle Laiduc, and Margarita Azmitia, "'You Never Become Fully Independent': Family Roles and Independence in First-Generation College Students," *Journal of Adolescent Research* 34, no. 4 (August 3, 2018): 381–410. https://doi .org/10.1177/0743558418788402.

Chapter 20

College Students with Young Kids—Especially Mothers—Find Themselves in a Time Crunch

CLAIRE WLADIS, *City University of New York*

IN A 2021 STUDY OF 11,195 US COLLEGE students, we found that college students who have children had significantly less time for college than their childless peers—about 4.3 hours less per week, to be specific.[1] This "time poverty" is greatest for mothers of preschool-age children.

Our study found other trends as well. Student parents also often had to care for children while they were studying. The most "time-poor" parents sacrificed a great deal more of their free time for their studies than did childless students who had more time and could complete an academic degree more rapidly.

Among all student parents, those with the youngest children—and mothers in particular—had the least time for college and were likelier to enroll in college part-time. For example, parents with children less than a year old spent a higher proportion of their free time—that is, time left over after all necessary tasks—on their education than any other group. This was perhaps an attempt to make up for the fact that they had less time for their studies.

In addition, despite having less available time for their studies in the first place, mothers on average spent more time on their education than fathers. For example, among parents with children ages one to five, mothers had 8.4 fewer hours per week to spend on their studies than fathers with children

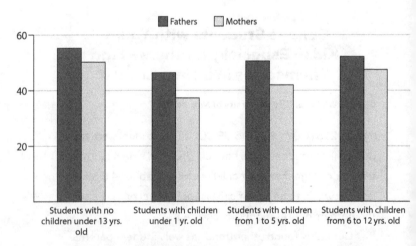

Hours per week that college students have for studying. Mothers with very young children reported having roughly nine fewer hours per week to study than did fathers of same-aged children.
The Conversation, CC-BY-ND. Data from Claire Wladis

of the same age. Still, these mothers spent almost two more hours per week on their education than fathers.

Why It Matters

This time difference matters because college students with children are more likely to drop out and take longer to complete their degrees than college students without children, even though on average they have higher GPAs, according to a study we published in 2018.[2]

In our 2021 study, having less time for college explained much of the difference in time spent on education between college students who have children and those who don't, as well as between mothers and fathers. It also explained differences among these groups in part-time enrollment.

However, mothers and fathers who lived with other adult family members who could help with childcare were able to devote more time to their college work. They also spent less time studying while simultaneously caring for children, and they enrolled in college full-time more often. Each additional adult family member living with a student parent increased the time they spent on their studies by over 1.5 hours each week. It also increased the time that student parents spent studying without children present by five percentage points and their probability of enrolling full-time by over two percentage points. This suggests that access to childcare is critical to the progress of student parents.

Improving outcomes for student parents is important not just for the students but for their children as well. One reason for this is that achieving a college degree is linked to better economic and educational outcomes for their children.

What Still Isn't Known

We don't yet know which kinds of supports might work best to improve outcomes for college students who are parents, but there are several potential solutions.

On-campus childcare at colleges in the United States currently serves only about 5% of student parents' needs and has declined over the last several decades. One possible approach could be to invest more systematically in on-campus childcare centers at colleges to support student parents. Another approach could be to increase federal financial aid awards to automatically cover the costs of childcare that student parents need in order to study or attend class.

What's Next

Time poverty may also be a challenge for students who are not parents. Since researching student parents, we have explored time poverty rates for other groups, including students who enroll in online courses, women, and students of color. We found that students who chose to enroll in online courses had higher time poverty and that this partially explained their worse college outcomes.[3]

We also found that Black, Hispanic, and female students had significantly higher rates of time poverty compared with other groups and that this revealed hidden gender inequities and explained a significant proportion of outcome gaps by race/ethnicity.[4] Furthermore, we found that the most time-poor groups actually sacrificed a higher proportion of their already limited free time for college. This suggests that time poverty may also contribute to other inequities, like less time for sleep and higher rates of burnout. More research is sorely needed to test which supports most effectively equalize time inequities and provide every student with the time that they need for college.

Notes

1. Katherine M. Conway, Claire Wladis, and Alyse C. Hachey, "Time Poverty and Parenthood: Who Has Time for College?," *AERA Open* 7 (May 19, 2021). https://doi.org/10.1177/23328584211011608.
2. Claire Wladis, Alyse C. Hachey, and Katherine Conway, "No Time for College? An Investigation of Time Poverty and Parenthood," *Journal of Higher Education* 89, no. 6 (May 30, 2018): 807–31. https://doi.org/10.1080/00221546.2018.1442983.
3. Claire Wladis, Alyse C. Hachey, and Katherine Conway, "Time Poverty: A Hidden Factor Connecting Online Enrollment and College Outcomes?," *Journal of Higher Education* 94, no. 5 (November 14, 2022): 609–37. https://doi.org/10.1080/00221546.2022.2138385.
4. Claire Wladis, Alyse C. Hachey, and Katherine M. Conway, "It's about Time, Part II: Does Time Poverty Contribute to Inequitable College Outcomes by Gender and Race/Ethnicity?," *AERA Open* 10 (March 2024). https://doi.org/10.1177/23328584241237971.

Chapter 21

More Solutions Needed for Campus Hunger

SUZANNA M. MARTINEZ, *University of California, San Francisco*

A FEDERAL REPORT RELEASED IN 2019 does a good job of explaining what many researchers have been saying for a decade—food insecurity among college students is a serious national problem.[1]

As one student from the University of California, Berkeley, revealed in an interview for a 2019 research article that I helped write: "Food is always on my mind: 'Do I have enough money? Maybe I should skip a meal today so I can have enough food for dinner.'"[2]

When it comes to offering up solutions, however, the 2019 report from the Government Accountability Office comes up short.

My experience researching campus hunger goes back to 2014, when colleagues and I conducted the first survey of campus hunger across a state's public university system. We found that over 40% of University of California students—about half of all undergraduates and one out of every four graduate students—faced food insecurity.[3] That is more than three times the 2022 national household rate of 12.8%. Food security is generally defined as having access at all times to enough food for an active, healthy life.

Our findings on campus hunger have been replicated in the University of California system, the California State University system, and in other colleges across the nation.[4]

Effects of an Empty Stomach

For those who are food secure, it might be easy to scoff at the notion that somehow college students can't find enough to eat. The reality is that hunger among college students has psychological impacts affecting their performance in school.

For instance, in a study published in 2020, colleagues and I found that students experiencing food insecurity had a lower grade point average than students not facing food insecurity. Researchers and I also found that not having access to enough food at all times increased a student's risk for poor mental health. This, in turn, increases their risk for lower grades.[5]

So what does the federal report—released 10 years after the first study documenting hunger on campus—say about the problem and what should be done about it?

The report stated that from 9% to more than 50% of America's college students face food insecurity. The report also revealed that of the two to three million students at risk for food insecurity who were potentially eligible for participating in the Supplemental Nutrition Assistance Program—more commonly known as SNAP—only 43% were receiving those benefits.

More Solutions Needed

The report recommended that government administrators do more to make students aware of their potential eligibility for SNAP benefits. The low participation rate in SNAP may stem from a lack of awareness of exemptions for eligibility. Or it could have to do with the stigma of receiving food assistance. Some organizations recommend campus-based initiatives to combat food insecurity in order to lessen the stigma associated with receiving food assistance for students. We tested the latter in the 10-campus University of California system, where campus basic-needs staff are trained to do SNAP outreach and application assistance for students. We interviewed these staff and found that SNAP student rules are challenging for students as well as the heterogeneity in how California county agencies interpret student exemptions.

Will better SNAP guidance end student hunger? In my view, as one who has been looking at this issue for some time, the answer is not completely, not until we end the student rule. For example, college students cannot get SNAP benefits unless they meet certain criteria, such as working at least 20 hours a week and attending school full-time. This rule should perhaps be rethought in light of how difficult it is to go to school full-time, keep up one's grades, and work more than 20 hours a week.

In a study I published with colleagues in 2024, California county agency workers who process students' applications in nine counties discussed the administrative burden involved in processing students' applications as well as inconsistencies in the process and training regarding the student rules. Their sentiments were to end the student SNAP rules.[6]

The Consolidated Appropriations Act of 2021 made it easier for college students to access SNAP, but federal modifications expired in 2023. In 2023, California enacted Assembly Bill 396, which enlists California's public higher education systems to certify academic programs as training and employment programs with the state in order to exempt participating students from the rule requiring student work. This could streamline student eligibility. At the federal level, the Enhance Access to SNAP Act, introduced in Congress in 2023, would allow for the pursuit of postsecondary credentials (if enrolled at least half-time) to be considered work participation for the purpose of SNAP eligibility.[7]

What else can we do to fix student hunger? Updating financial aid for college students is one solution. There was a US$500 increase to the maximum federal Pell Grant in 2023, and the Biden administration has proposed a 10% increase from current levels. Another solution is to extend the National School Lunch Program, which could help to take up slack in the lost purchasing power of the Pell Grant.

In my view, more assistance should also be given to graduate students, who face campus hunger too but who were not mentioned in the 2019 federal report.

Lastly, students must be better educated on things such as financial aid, personal budgeting, and self-advocacy. At a time when the cost of going to college is becoming more difficult to cover, it's more important than ever to help students succeed and be healthy so that they can lead future generations.

Notes

1. *Food Insecurity: Better Information Could Help Eligible College Students Access Federal Food Assistance Benefits*, US Government Accountability Office, December 21, 2018. https://www.gao.gov/products/gao-19-95.
2. Anthony Meza, Emily Altman, Suzanna Martinez, and Cindy W. Leung, "'It's a Feeling That One Is Not Worth Food': A Qualitative Study Exploring the Psychosocial Experience and Academic Consequences of Food Insecurity among College Students," *Journal of the Academy of Nutrition and Dietetics* 119, no. 10 (October 2019): 1713–21. https://doi.org/10.1016/j.jand.2018.09.006.
3. Suzanna M. Martinez, Karen Webb, Edward A. Frongillo, and Lorrene D. Ritchie, "Food Insecurity in California's Public University System: What Are the Risk Factors?," *Journal of Hunger & Environmental Nutrition* 13, no. 1 (November 21, 2017): 1–18. https://doi.org/10.1080/19320248.2017.1374901.
4. Aydin Nazmi, Suzanna Martinez, Ajani Byrd, Derrick Robinson, Stephanie Bianco, Jennifer Maguire, Rashida M. Crutchfield, Kelly Condron, and Lorrene Ritchie, "A Systematic Review of Food Insecurity among US Students in Higher Education," *Journal of Hunger & Environmental Nutrition* 14, no. 5 (June 22, 2018): 725–40. https://doi.org/10.1080/19320248.2018.1484316.
5. Suzanna M. Martinez, Edward A. Frongillo, Cindy Leung, and Lorrene Ritchie, "No Food for Thought: Food Insecurity Is Related to Poor Mental Health and Lower Academic Performance among Students in California's Public University System," *Journal of Health Psychology* 25, no. 12 (2020): 1930–939.
6. Suzanna M. Martinez, Sonali Singh, Erin Esaryk, and Lorrene Ritchie, "SNAP Student Rules Are Not So Snappy: Lessons Learned from a Qualitative Study of California County Agency Workers," *Journal of Nutrition Education and Behavior* 56, no. 3 (March 2024): 133–44. https://doi.org/10.1016/j.jneb.2023.12.004.
7. S.1488—EATS Act of 2023, 118th Congress. https://www.congress.gov/bill/118th-congress/senate-bill/1488#:~:text=Specifically%2C%20the%20bill%20removes%20the,time%20to%20participate%20in%20SNAP.

Chapter 22

As Second Chance Pell Grant Program Grows, More Incarcerated People Can Get Degrees

MNEESHA GELLMAN, *Emerson College*

PEOPLE IN PRISON RARELY get to go to college. While more than 53% of US adults have a college degree or other postsecondary certificate, only 15% of incarcerated people have such credentials. But an expansion in access to federal financial aid through Pell Grants for those who are incarcerated is making higher education a bit more available.

Joshua Dankoff, who directs strategic initiatives at the nonprofit Citizens for Juvenile Justice, collects data on prison education. He found that in Massachusetts, where I live, nearly 2,000 of the 5,300 people in custody with the Department of Correction are on college or vocational education wait lists. Only 213 are enrolled in some form of postsecondary education. Just 77 are enrolled in a bachelor's program.[1]

The reason that so few US prisons offer college education stems from a 1994 crime bill that banned federal financial aid to people in prison.

The Second Chance Pell experiment, launched by the Obama administration in 2015, reinstated Pell Grants for incarcerated students who are eligible for a grant. To apply for a Pell, students must qualify by filing the Free Application for Federal Student Aid, or FAFSA, and be enrolled in college through a Pell-eligible institution while in prison. The program initially covered just 67 programs. An additional 67 were added in 2020.

The Biden administration expanded Second Chance Pell access by adding 73 schools in 2023, including 24 historically Black colleges and universities. As of July 2023, more than 200 higher education programs will serve incarcerated students with Pell support.[2]

As the director of the Emerson Prison Initiative at Emerson College, I believe it's important to distinguish between the different educational programs offered within prisons. There are three main types. The first is high school equivalency and vocational programs run by departments of correction. The second is educational non-credit-bearing programs offered by outside volunteer organizations, such as gardening clubs or Toastmasters. The third is credit-bearing degree programs run by outside colleges and universities, like mine.

Prison-Run Education Programs

Most US states, such as California, New York, and Massachusetts, provide adult basic education, or ABE, to incarcerated people. Some also mandate access to English-language instruction. ABE is meant to improve literacy and numeracy and offer the opportunity for incarcerated people to get a high school equivalency diploma. Many prisons also offer computer classes and other supplemental non-credit-bearing courses.

Educational opportunities like these are "prison education."[3] The programs are designed and carried out by correctional staff. Although prison education programs may strive for universal benchmarks such as passing HiSET or GED high school equivalency tests, the guidelines for who can participate are set by prison administrators in partnership with state agencies.

For example, in Massachusetts, the Department of Elementary and Secondary Education provides curricular standards and funding for ABE and testing both within and outside prison. And while the state Department of Correction received funding for just under 200 ABE spots per year in recent years, it did not request funding for the next five years, suggesting that fewer people will have access to prison education.

Furthermore, while incarcerated young people under age 22 with an identified disability and no high school diploma have a right to special education services, Dankoff analyzed Massachusetts data and found that only a fraction of young people in this situation actually received these services.[4] This is largely because jails and prisons do a poor job of identifying young people with special education needs. It is also because systems of incarceration are oriented toward punishment rather than education.

College-Run Programs in Prison

Some prisons allow education programming through outside partnerships with colleges and universities. Students in "college in prison" programs are usually enrolled in college-level degree-granting programs that lead to certificates, associate degrees, or bachelor degrees. These are the types of programs that can grow under the Pell Grant expansion.

Many colleges and universities that bring their programming inside prison walls try to provide an education for incarcerated students that is comparable to what they provide traditional college students. Educators from the outside come into the prison to teach. The programs often offer library research support, accessibility services, and academic advising as well—in line with best practices for colleges in general. They must adapt, however, to censorship restrictions within prisons, as well as limited internet and technology access, along with a host of additional regulations.

Power of Language

In my experience, many prison educators are dedicated to the transformational power of education, just like their college-in-prison counterparts.

A small, but I believe important difference, between the two is that prison-run programs typically refer to incarcerated students as *prisoners* or *inmates*, continuing a language choice of departments of correction. In contrast, programs like the Emerson Prison Initiative refer to the people we work with as *students*, *applicants*, or *students who are incarcerated*. This language treats incarcerated students with respect and dignity, and also grants them a non-carceral identity, which I argue is central to student success and well-being.[5]

The expansion of Pell Grants to more incarcerated people offers an opportunity to make college in prison more widely available, while also maintaining best practices in this rapidly growing field. Such practices include little things, like the labels we use to refer to students, and big things, like ensuring that those who draw Pell Grants enroll in rigorous programs where they get a quality education and earn a degree.

Notes

1. *Unlocking College: Strengthening Massachusetts' Commitment to College in Prison*, Boston Foundation, October 2022. https://www.tbf.org/-/media/tbf/reports-and-covers/2022/november/unlocking-college-report.pdf.
2. Melanie Hanson, "Pell Grant Statistics," EducationData.org, January 28, 2024. https://educationdata.org/pell-grant-statistics.
3. Meagan Wilson, Rayane Alamuddin, and Danielle Cooper, "Unbarring Access: A Landscape Review of Postsecondary Education in Prison and Its Pedagogical Supports," Ithaka S+R, May 30, 2019. https://doi.org/10.18665/sr.311499.
4. *School's Out: Massachusetts Youth in Adult Correctional Systems Denied Education*, Citizens for Juvenile Justice, August 2022, https://static1.squarespace.com/static/58ea378e414fb5fae5ba06c7/t/638f6db0d425c16e5fdb58d5/1670344113438/SchoolsOut.pdf.
5. Mneesha Gellman, ed., *Education behind the Wall: Why and How We Teach College in Prison* (Waltham, MA: Brandeis University Press, 2022).

Part V.

The Importance of Diversity

Although universities in the United States excel at educating the global elite, they often struggle to provide the same level of education to the country's resident population. When college is framed as a private good, wealthy students reap the benefits, and inequity gaps in society increase. The chapters in part V make a case for the continued importance of diversity in higher education.

A college education is often presented as the great equalizer, as the best way for a person to move from poverty into the middle class. With the elimination of affirmative action for race-based admissions, some institutions are making other efforts to close equity gaps. One solution for institutions is hiring more faculty and staff of color. As Bowman shows, gaps in the college graduation rates between different racial/ethnic groups of students tend to shrink when there are more faculty of color on campus.

Another strategy that institutions have employed in closing equity gaps between groups of students on campus is instituting diversity programs like those discussed by Licht. Creating an environment where all students, faculty, and staff can flourish requires reviewing policies and procedures with an equity-minded approach. Many institutions conduct equity audits of existing policies for student retention and progress as well as those for hiring, developing, and promoting faculty and staff.

Equity work at our institutions is often invisible, and as Misra, Kuvaeva, Jaeger, Culpepper, and O'Meara explain, this work is more often done by women faculty and faculty of color. For women faculty of color, this workload is the heaviest. It includes mentoring students and junior faculty and also serving on committees, work that doesn't always count toward tenure and promotion. Equity audits are commonly used to redistribute workloads more equitably and to make this distribution more transparent.

A potentially more radical strategy to support equity and diversity on our campuses is the practice of hiring a woman of color as the leader of the institution. Having a woman of color in the president's role can be a strong signal that an institution supports diversity. Organizational scholars like Commodore have written about the importance of bringing diverse lived experiences and perspectives to the creation of innovative solutions.

As Commodore highlights, having a woman in the president's role is a sign to our female students, faculty members, staff members, and alumni that they too could become a university leader. When institutions focus on diversity and equity practices, from striving for equitable graduation rates to changing the face of the college presidency, they are committing to creating a more racially and economically just society.

Chapter 23

How Colleges Seek to Increase Racial Diversity without Relying on Race in College Admissions

LAUREN FOLEY, *Western Michigan University*

WHEN THE US SUPREME COURT OUTLAWED the use of racial identity in college admissions in June 2023, it forced colleges and universities to rethink how to maintain and increase diversity in their student bodies. This is a topic that I, a political science professor, explore in my book *On the Basis of Race: How Higher Education Navigates Affirmative Action Policies.*[1] Below, I expound on what I see as the future of diversity in higher education, now that college admission officials can no longer consider race.

Is Racial Diversity in Higher Education about to Suffer?

The likelihood is that admission for racial minority students will suffer as a result of the nationwide affirmative action ban precipitated by the case *Students for Fair Admissions v. Harvard.*[2] We know this from research done in states with existing bans on affirmative action. Courts and ballot initiatives have banned affirmative action by state in the last three decades. These states include California in 1996,[3] Washington in 1998, Michigan in 2006, Nebraska in 2008, and Arizona in 2010. In 1996 the US Court of Appeals for the Fifth Circuit, in its decision on *Hopwood v. Texas*, banned affirmative action across its jurisdiction: Texas, Mississippi, and Louisiana.

Regardless of how selective a public university may be, the enrollment of racial minorities declines at public universities if they are located in states that ban affirmative action.[4] The largest effects are felt at the most selective flagship universities, like the University of California, Berkeley; the University of California, Los Angeles; and the University of Michigan. All of these schools self-reported dramatic declines in minority representation, particularly among Black, Hispanic, and Native students. According to this data, underrepresented groups declined by 12% across the University of California system. At the University of Michigan, Black and Native undergraduate enrollment fell by 44% and 90%, respectively, in the years following the affirmative action ban.

Affirmative action was a precise tool in that it allowed universities to pay attention to specific populations of applicants. Without this tool, universities are left with blunt policy solutions and thus struggle to maintain student racial diversity.

A ban on the method is not a ban on the goal, however. Nationally, universities can no longer practice affirmative action as a way to maintain racial diversity among their students, but this does not mean that universities will abandon their commitment to racial diversity. Even in states that already had bans on affirmative action before the Supreme Court banned the practice, universities reiterated their commitment to racial diversity.[5] They also reaffirmed that they would both comply with the ban and find ways to prioritize diversity.

Still, I believe that banning affirmative action could have a chilling effect on the willingness of some universities to explicitly mention race in their positions and policies on diversity and inclusion. Bans on affirmative action discourage university administrators from using race as a criterion in admissions, even when they are otherwise allowed to do so; universities that are less selective have adopted broader statements about diversity and student recruitment that do not explicitly mention race.[6]

How Are Colleges Responding?

When colleges use race-neutral strategies to increase racial diversity, they don't get the same results that they did with race-conscious affirmative action. There simply are no policy tools that work as well as affirmative action at producing racial diversity. Nevertheless, universities will now seek out race-neutral methods to maintain or increase racial diversity on campus.

One example is holistic admissions. This involves assessing an applicant's academic achievements using multiple factors. These factors include socioeconomic hardship, educational disadvantages, or other forms of adversity.

Computer software can aid universities in making demographic factors part of application review, such as the educational backgrounds of an applicant's parents, the number of students on free or reduced-price lunch at the schools that the applicant attended, and the socioeconomic status of the applicant's family.

Other states have tried legislative solutions, such as guaranteeing acceptance at state universities to resident applicants whose GPA puts them in a top-tier percentage of their graduating class.[7]

Following the *Students for Fair Admissions v. Harvard* ruling, some colleges and universities have pursued creative solutions to comply with the Supreme Court's decision. For example, at Sarah Lawrence College, the admission application cites language from the decision when it asks students to comment on the role that race has played in their lives.

Notes

1. Lauren S. Foley, *On the Basis of Race: How Higher Education Navigates Affirmative Action Policies* (New York: New York University Press, 2023).
2. Grant H. Blume and Mark C. Long, "Changes in Levels of Affirmative Action in College Admissions in Response to Statewide Bans and Judicial Rulings," *Educational Evaluation and Policy Analysis* 36, no. 2 (June 1, 2014): 228–52. https://doi.org/10.3102/0162373713508810.
3. Caitlin Knowles Myers, "A Cure for Discrimination? Affirmative Action and the Case of California's Proposition 209," *ILR Review* 60, no. 3 (April 2007): 379–96. https://doi.org/10.1177/001979390706000304.
4. Huacong Liu, "How Do Affirmative Action Bans Affect the Racial Composition of Postsecondary Students in Public Institutions?," *Educational Policy* 36, no. 6 (October 1, 2020): 1348–72. https://doi.org/10.1177/0895904820961007.
5. Jerome Karabel, "The Rise and Fall of Affirmative Action at the University of California," *Journal of Blacks in Higher Education*, no. 25 (Autumn 1999): 109–12. https://doi.org/10.2307/2999406.

6. Eric Grodsky and Demetra Kalogrides, "The Declining Significance of Race in College Admissions Decisions," *American Journal of Education* 115, no. 1 (November 2008): 1–33. https://doi.org/10.1086 /590673.
7. Sunny Xinchun Niu and Marta Tienda, "The Impact of the Texas Top 10 Percent Law on College Enrollment: A Regression Discontinuity Approach," *Journal of Policy Analysis and Management* 29, no. 1 (Winter 2010): 84–110. https://doi.org/10.1002/pam.20480.

Chapter 24

More Student or Faculty Diversity on Campus Leads to Lower Racial Gaps in Graduation Rates

NICHOLAS A. BOWMAN, *University of Iowa*

COLLEGE GRADUATION GAPS between Black and white students tend to shrink when there are more students of color or faculty of color on campus. This finding is based on analyses of 2,807 four-year US colleges conducted by psychology researcher Nida Denson and me, published in 2022.[1]

Not only did we find that the gap in graduation rates between Black and white students is smaller at colleges with a larger percentage of Black students or faculty. We also found that the presence of one racial group may lead to smaller graduation gaps for other groups as well. For example, a greater percentage of Black students or instructors often helps shrink the graduation gap between other groups, such as Latino and white students.

Our findings mainly came from colleges where almost no students attend online programs. Students in online coursework sometimes know the race of their instructor and other students. However, these racial identities may not be obvious in online courses on a day-to-day basis, especially if students have few chances to interact.

In addition, at colleges and universities with a majority-Black student population, Black students have the same graduation rates as white students. This same pattern is also

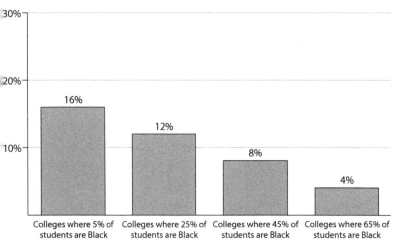

The graduation gap shrinks as the portion of Black students increases. In schools where 5% of the students were Black, white students were 16% more likely than Black students to graduate. In colleges where 65% of the students were Black, white students were only 4% more likely to graduate than Black students.
The Conversation, CC-BY-ND. Data from Nicholas A. Bowman

seen for Latino and white students at colleges with a majority-Latino population.

Our findings hold even after we took other factors into account, such as how selective the college was, where it was located, and how much it cost to attend.

Why It Matters

College graduation rates vary substantially across racial groups. For instance, white students who began attending a four-year college in 2010 graduated within six years at a rate of 63.9%, whereas Black students who began college the same year graduated at a rate of 39.7%, federal data shows.[2]

Our research highlights an overlooked reason that may explain some of these gaps: the presence of a large majority of white students and faculty at many colleges. This finding is important because colleges often have some control over the students whom they choose to recruit and admit as well as the faculty they hire.

Our finding that majority-Black and majority-Latino colleges have managed to eliminate gaps in graduation rates—despite centuries of past and present racism that affect student outcomes—is also notable. Some of these colleges have a founding mission of supporting students of color, such as historically Black colleges and universities, which were originally created for Black students who were prevented from attending white colleges. Others have a large percentage of students of color without this type of history, such as California State University, Fresno.

Receiving a college degree provides benefits in terms of future employment, income, mental well-being, physical health, and civic participation.[3] Additionally, a well-educated population provides economic, health, and civic benefits to society overall.[4] Therefore, promoting equitable graduation rates serves as one critical step in the effort toward creating a more racially just society.

Future research is needed to better understand how and why the presence of students and faculty of color may lead to equitable graduation rates. Moreover, colleges and universities may want to bolster their efforts to hire faculty of color to improve their students' outcomes.

What Still Isn't Known

While this study shows that higher percentages of students and faculty of color tend to close racial gaps in graduation rates, it does not explain how this happens. This closing of gaps may occur from students of color feeling comfort when seeing other people of color on campus, having more interactions and friendships with students of color, or experiencing more inclusive classroom environments with faculty members of color.

Notes

1. Nicholas A. Bowman and Nida Denson, "Institutional Racial Representation and Equity Gaps in College Graduation," *Journal of Higher Education* 93, no. 3 (September 10, 2021): 399–423. https://doi.org/10.1080/00221546.2021.1971487.
2. Table 326.10, "Digest of Education Statistics," National Center of Education Statistics, 2017. https://nces.ed.gov/programs/digest/d17/tables/dt17_326.10.asp?referer=raceindicators.
3. Matthew J. Mayhew, Alyssa N. Rockenbach, Nicholas A. Bowman, Tricia A. Seifert, and Gregory C. Wolniak with Ernest T. Pascarella and Patrick T. Terenzini, *How College Affects Students: 21st Century Evidence That Higher Education Works*, vol. 3 (San Francisco: Jossey-Bass, 2016).
4. Michael Hout, "Social and Economic Returns to College Education in the United States," *Annual Review of Sociology* 38, no. 1 (August 2012): 379–400. https://doi.org/10.1146/annurev.soc.012809.102503.

Chapter 25

5 Ways That College Campuses Benefit from Diversity, Equity, and Inclusion Programs

ERICA JACQUELINE LICHT, *Harvard Kennedy School*

FOR MORE THAN HALF A CENTURY, colleges and universities have relied on dedicated programs to attract students of color and support them.[1] Since their inception, those programs—known as diversity, equity, and inclusion, or DEI, programs—have been under attack. This assault continued to balloon even more significantly following 2020's national racial justice protests and the subsequent increase in such programs.

Republican lawmakers assail the programs as being driven by the "woke agenda" of liberal Democrats aimed at valuing and prioritizing racial identity over merit. Rigorous social science research shows, however, that these programs result in universities with better student learning.[2]

As a researcher who is concerned with racial equity on campus, I contend there are five ways that DEI programs have made a positive difference at US colleges and universities.

1. Students Perform Better Academically

Students from marginalized identity groups—including Black, Indigenous, Latinx, and Asian students as well as first-generation students—perform better academically at schools with diversity programs, and they graduate at a higher rate.[3]

As a result of DEI programs, students also report feeling more included on campus through dedicated resources and spaces for students of color. This sense of belonging also increases when, as a part of DEI programs, more faculty of color are hired. When students feel like they belong, they stay in school and graduate after four years at a higher rate than those who do not.

2. Students Are Less Biased

DEI programs have been shown to create more racially diverse learning environments. These more diverse environments have proven to reduce bias and promote peer acceptance. Increased contact between students from different racial groups results in increased understanding of different perspectives and development of trust. Students of color also report having less racial stress,[4] and they attest to having fewer feelings of imposter syndrome on campus.[5]

3. More Satisfied Faculty

Faculty at schools with DEI programs that include mentorship tend to stay at their jobs longer and are more satisfied at the workplace. This increased job satisfaction owes to how DEI programs restructure university policies on hiring, promotion, and advancement.[6] This restructuring includes redesigning job descriptions, including more voices in the interview process, and requiring implicit bias training for search committees. Additionally, these changes result in increasing the number of junior faculty of color on campus.

4. More Engaging Curriculum and Classrooms

DEI programs produce more engaged scholarship, which results in a higher quality of curriculum and of classroom learning as reported by students themselves.[7] Faculty on campuses with greater curricular innovation publish higher-quality work on issues that affect the communities in which their students will live and work. Engaged academic work connects classroom learning to issues that students experience directly themselves, such as racism and discrimination based on class, gender, and sexuality.

5. Students Are More Prepared to Be Local Leaders

As a result of DEI programs, students are more engaged in their communities after they graduate.[8] They are more likely to participate in local government and politics, including turning out to vote and running for office after graduation. Graduating students at schools with DEI programs are also more likely to have interracial friendships and are more prepared for multiracial professional settings because they gain a better understanding of race and ethnicity.

DEI programs have been time-tested in changing campuses for the better and attracting more Black, Indigenous, Latinx, and Asian students. Since race-based admissions were outlawed by a decision of the US Supreme Court in 2023, DEI efforts can play an even greater role in attracting more students of color and creating the conditions for them to thrive.

Notes

1. Shannon L. Avery-Desmarais, Susan M. Hunter Revell, and Mary K. McCurry, "A Theoretical Framework to Promote Minority PhD and DNP Student Success in Nursing Education," *Journal of Professional Nursing* 37, no. 6 (2021): 1149–53. https://doi.org/10.1016/j.profnurs .2021.10.002; Alan M. Schwitzer, Oris T. Griffin, Julie R. Ancis, and Celeste R. Thomas, "Social Adjustment Experiences of African American College Students," *Journal of Counseling & Development* 77, no. 2 (1999): 189–97. https://doi.org/10.1002/j.1556-6676.1999 .tb02439.x.
2. Daryl G. Smith and Natalie B. Schonfeld, "The Benefits of Diversity: What the Research Tells Us," *About Campus: Enriching the Student Learning Experience* 5, no. 5 (2000): 16–23. https://doi.org/10.1177 /108648220000500505.
3. Vernon R. Padgett and John F. Reid, "Five Year Evaluation of the Student Diversity Program: A Retrospective Quasi-experiment," *Journal of College Student Retention: Research, Theory & Practice* 4, no. 2 (August 2002): 135–45. https://doi.org/10.2190/25t7-3bbf -6hyb-nhay.
4. Kevin Cokley, Shannon McClain, Alicia Enciso, and Mercedes Martinez, "An Examination of the Impact of Minority Status Stress and Impostor Feelings on the Mental Health of Diverse Ethnic Minority College Students," *Journal of Multicultural Counseling and Development* 41, no. 2 (April 8, 2013): 82–95. https://doi.org/10.1002/j.2161-1912.2013 .00029.x.
5. Bridgette J. Peteet, LaTrice Montgomery, and Jerren C. Weekes, "Predictors of Imposter Phenomenon among Talented Ethnic Minority Undergraduate Students," *Journal of Negro Education* 84, no. 2

(Spring 2015): 175–86. https://doi.org/10.7709/jnegroeducation.84.2
.0175.

6. Román Liera, "Moving beyond a Culture of Niceness in Faculty Hiring to Advance Racial Equity," *American Educational Research Journal* 57, no. 5 (December 6, 2019): 1954–94. https://doi.org/10.3102 /0002831219888624.

7. Susan Strum, Timothy Eatman, John Saltmarch, and Adam Bush, "Full Participation: Building the Architecture for Diversity and Community Engagement in Higher Education," 2011, SURFACE: Syracuse University open access repository. https://surface.syr.edu/cgi /viewcontent.cgi?article=1001&context=ia.

8. Nicholas A. Bowman, "Promoting Participation in a Diverse Democracy: A Meta-analysis of College Diversity Experiences and Civic Engagement," *Review of Educational Research* 81, no. 1 (March 1, 2011): 29–68. https://doi.org/10.3102/0034654310383047.

Chapter 26

3 Ways to Make "Belonging" More Than a Buzzword

MICHELLE SAMURA, *Santiago Canyon College*

BELONGING IS TRENDING.

You can see it in evolving executive titles, such as "vice president of global diversity, inclusion and belonging." You can find it in reports about how to make employees feel they're a more essential part of the workplace. For instance, a 2021 report about trends in the workplace found that belonging is a key factor in how companies keep employees engaged. And it can be seen in new "belonging" initiatives and strategies to create an environment of belonging and develop more inclusivity across organizations of all sorts.

But what about on a college campus? Does the recent increased interest in belonging help students? Might it carry unintended consequences?

As a researcher who concentrates on factors that influence belonging among college students, I decided to probe more deeply into the focus on belonging and its relationship to how college students fare. In my research, I define belonging as a concept of people's connectedness and their view of mattering at the institutions or organizations where they work, study, or are otherwise involved. Will this emphasis on belonging actually enhance students' well-being and ultimately help them succeed? Or is it just being used as a feel-good buzzword that is meant to appease recent demands for greater inclusion?

A Crucial Need

There's no shortage of research that has identified belonging as a critical need for human beings,[1] especially for college students. Studies have found that belonging is a key to college student success.[2] Belonging is associated with students not dropping out of school,[3] with their psychologically adjusting to college,[4] and with their academic achievement. Belonging is especially important for students of color who attend institutions that were not designed with them in mind.[5]

While most research about belonging on campus has focused on how students interact with other people, my own research has examined how campus spaces—such as residence halls and classrooms—can enhance student belonging. I've found that the design of campus spaces can increase the frequency of interactions among students. If those interactions are positive, they can then lead to belonging. I've also found that where students go on campus—or don't go, for that matter—says a lot about when and with whom they experience belonging.

I don't question that belonging on campus is an important consideration. Rather, I'm suggesting that people question generally accepted ways of talking about belonging. Here are three alternative ways to think about it.

1. Belonging Is an Ongoing Process

Phrases such as *sense of belonging* are commonly used in discussions about belonging. This language suggests that belonging is a feeling or a state of being, but it's actually more than that. Even how belonging is measured can perpetuate a view that one's belonging remains constant and consistent, overlooking the fact that "belonging" can fluctuate over time. Belonging among college students often is measured through surveys, but surveys are only snapshots.

Beyond shifts in belonging at different times, students may also experience belonging differently in different places and with different people.[6] For example, I found that students at one university identified the dining hall as a key site to connect with their friends. It was a space that represented their belonging. For other students, however, the same dining hall was a stressful place. For these students, it was a space that made them feel isolated.

Instead of viewing belonging as a feeling or a sense, consider how belonging is an ongoing process. In my 2016 study of college students' belonging, I found that when students' expectations for their academic and social lives did not match what they encountered during college, they indicated having lower belonging academically and socially.[7] To change that, students would seek out different places on campus and rethink their own views of themselves. They would also form new clubs for students and seek places on campus for those groups to meet.

The takeaway is that even if someone doesn't belong at first, it doesn't mean they won't belong in the future.

2. Belonging Takes Effort

When belonging is seen as fitting in, it's easy for people to assume that individuals can fit or even want to fit. It's also easy to make assumptions about who belongs where or with whom. This view can lead to expectations about what conditions promote belonging, such as being around people who are alike. However, being around people who are seen as being alike isn't always associated with belonging, however.

In a study on belonging at a multicampus university system, I found that Asian American students at a university where they were relatively few in number reported higher levels of belonging than did Asian American students at campuses with much larger Asian American student populations.[8] Findings indicated that student belonging may not require being around people from the same racial or ethnic group. Belonging can occur among difference. So it's useful for colleges to question people's thinking about who belongs with whom.

The study's findings also revealed that Asian American students actively sought out spaces and groups with whom they shared similar interests or thought they could relate, such as a speech and debate club, cultural organizations, and the recreation center for pickup basketball. In these cases,

belonging didn't just occur by itself. Students had to deliber-
ately seek it out.

3. Belonging Is a Shared Responsibility

People may view belonging as a personal matter—something
experienced at an individual level that is an individual's
responsibility. But it also requires ongoing effort by
organizations and institutions.

Colleges and universities can change their structures
and systems to support belonging and inclusion. This can
include giving attention to differences between what
colleges display in marketing materials and the reality of
what students experience on campus.[9] This can also include
investing in campus spaces and programs that facilitate
frequent, positive interactions among diverse students and
faculty.

In my experience, belonging is often thought of as a
condition that does not change and depends on the actions
of an individual student. What I've found through my research,
though, is that belonging on campus takes ongoing effort—
not only by students but by the colleges they attend as well.
By thinking about belonging in these different ways, the kinds
of change needed for greater student belonging may actually
happen.

Notes

1. Roy F. Baumeister and Mark R. Leary, "The Need to Belong: Desire for
   Interpersonal Attachments as a Fundamental Human Motivation,"
   Psychological Bulletin 117, no. 3 (1995): 497–529. https://doi.org/10
   .1037/0033-2909.117.3.497.
2. Terrell L. Strayhorn, *College Students' Sense of Belonging: A Key to
   Educational Success for All Students*, 2nd ed. (New York: Routledge,
   2018).

3. Marybeth Hoffman, Jayne Richmond, Jennifer Morrow, and Kandice Salomone, "Investigating 'Sense of Belonging' in First-Year College Students," *Journal of College Student Retention: Research, Theory & Practice* 4, no. 3 (November 2002): 227–56. https://doi.org/10.2190/dryc-cxq9-jq8v-ht4v.

4. Laura D. Pittman and Adeya Richmond, "University Belonging, Friendship Quality, and Psychological Adjustment during the Transition to College," *Journal of Experimental Education* 76, no. 4 (July 21, 2008): 343–62. https://doi.org/10.3200/jexe.76.4.343-362.

5. Sylvia Hurtado and Deborah Faye Carter, "Effects of College Transition and Perceptions of the Campus Racial Climate on Latino College Students' Sense of Belonging," *Sociology of Education* 70, no. 4 (October 1997): 324–45. https://doi.org/10.2307/2673270.

6. Michelle Samura, "Understanding Campus Spaces to Improve Student Belonging," *About Campus: Enriching the Student Learning Experience* 23, no. 2 (May 2018): 19–23. https://doi.org/10.1177/1086482218785887.

7. Michelle Samura, "Remaking Selves, Repositioning Selves, or Remaking Space: An Examination of Asian American College Students' Processes of 'Belonging,'" *Journal of College Student Development* 57, no. 2 (March 2016): 135–50. https://doi.org/10.1353/csd.2016.0016.

8. Michelle Samura, "How Do We Know If Asian American Students Feel Like They Belong on Our Campuses?," NASPA API Knowledge Community Blog. https://naspaapikc.wordpress.com/2013/10/17/how-do-we-know-if-asian-american-students-feel-like-they-belong-on-our-campuses-by-michelle-samura-ph-d-chapman-university/.

9. Michelle Samura, "A Tale of Two Settings: Rethinking Methods and Approaches for Diversity Research," *Humboldt Journal of Social Relations* 1, no. 39 (May 2017): 43–50. https://doi.org/10.55671/0160-4341.1008.

Chapter 27

Female Faculty of Color Do Extra Diversity Work for No Extra Reward—Here's How to Fix That

JOYA MISRA, *University of Massachusetts, Amherst*

ALEXANDRA KUVAEVA, *University of Maryland*

AUDREY J. JAEGER, *North Carolina State University*

DAWN KIYOE CULPEPPER, *University of Maryland*

KERRYANN O'MEARA, *Columbia University*

COLLEGE FACULTY MEMBERS are critical in helping American colleges become more diverse, inclusive, and equitable. Professors and instructors not only teach and advise students; they also help institutions make inroads toward equity goals, such as improving graduation rates for underrepresented students, by connecting with and serving as role models for students.

Female faculty members of color in particular are disproportionately called on by both colleagues and students to do diversity, equity, and inclusion work.[1] While diversity work is often meaningful to them, most faculty members' workload and reward system are not designed to recognize this labor when it comes to salary and promotion. This is just one example of how sexism and racism contribute to the persistent lack of female faculty members of color across higher education.

As researchers with the Faculty Workload and Rewards Project, which was funded by the National Science Foundation, our team analyzed workloads for 957 faculty members from 22 US colleges and universities. We identified how racial and gender inequalities lead to extra work and less recognition for female faculty members.[2]

The "Identity Tax"

Many faculty members struggle with balancing the different elements of their workload, in what might be referred to as "work–work balance."[3] In addition to teaching students, faculty members are expected to advise students, conduct research, and engage in administrative and leadership work. Yet although universities expect them to contribute in these ways, faculty members are rarely evaluated on all of these contributions. At universities with graduate programs and at selective liberal arts colleges, research is typically the primary focus, while teaching may be a bigger priority at colleges focused on undergraduate education.

As previous research has shown, white women and faculty members of color recognize that workloads are unfairly distributed among faculty.[4] For example, women are more likely to do work that supports the institution, such as mentoring students, revising the curriculum, or organizing departmental events. This work, however, is not generally rewarded in salary and promotion decisions. Male faculty members, on the other hand, are more likely to protect their research time, which is more likely to line up with how they are evaluated.

Faculty members of color, in particular, pay an "identity tax," which is exacerbated for women of color.[5] They are asked to do more mentoring of students—especially students of color—and to take on leadership and diversity work on campus. Although this work is less valued for promotion, faculty members of color report that these responsibilities can give their work special meaning.[6]

How to Make Workloads More Transparent

The goal of the Faculty Workload and Rewards Project was not merely to observe workload differences. We also identified a number of changes that departments can make to solve these workload inequities.

One solution is for colleges to make faculty workload measurements and expectations more transparent. For example, if women of color among faculty understand workload expectations for their position in terms of numbers of courses taught, students advised, and committee work done, they are more likely to feel credited for their work.[7] And if, for example, a faculty member is advising eight students when the clear norm is five, she will know she is overperforming and might decline taking on additional students.

Additionally, when women of color work in departments that assign teaching, advising, and administrative work systematically—for example, the department chair asks each faculty member to advise five students—they are less likely to see their work as devalued.

In both of these systems, faculty members know that their workload will be linked to how they are rewarded.

Crediting is another important part of making faculty workloads more equitable.

Workload equity does not require that every faculty member do the same job. Some faculty members prefer, for example, advising students, while others prefer committee work. Distributing workload equitably is different from distributing workload equally. Equitable workload systems can, for example, substitute more time advising students with less time serving on committees, and vice versa. This approach credits faculty members for their workload in ways that take into account their preferences and skill sets.

These are relatively simple fixes, but they can make a difference in how women of color feel about whether and how their workload is recognized by their colleagues.

The "Can of Worms Is Already Open"

As we worked with departments committed to addressing workload inequities, they compared implementing more transparency with opening a can of worms. Department chairs worry, for example, that faculty members will be more likely to complain that colleagues are not doing their share. Yet the can of worms is already open—and is having damaging effects on the careers of female faculty members of color.

Notes

1. Caroline Sotello Vierno Turner, "Women of Color in Academe: Living with Multiple Marginality," *Journal of Higher Education* 73, no. 1 (January 2002): 74–93. https://doi.org/10.1080/00221546.2002 .11777131.
2. Sarah Winslow, "Gender Inequality and Time Allocations among Academic Faculty," *Gender & Society* 24, no. 6 (2010): 769–93. https://doi.org/10.1177/0891243210386728.
3. Joya Misra, Jennifer Hickes Lundquist, and Abby Templer, "Gender, Work Time, and Care Responsibilities among Faculty," *Sociological Forum* 27, no. 2 (May 30, 2012): 300–323. https://doi.org/10.1111/j .1573-7861.2012.01319.x.
4. KerryAnn O'Meara, Audrey Jaeger, Joya Misra, Courtney Lennartz, and Alexandra Kuvaeva, "Undoing Disparities in Faculty Workloads: A Randomized Trial Experiment," *PLOS One* 13, no. 12 (December 19, 2018). https://doi.org/10.1371/journal.pone.0207316.
5. Laura E. Hirshfield and Tiffany D. Joseph, " 'We Need a Woman, We Need a Black Woman': Gender, Race, and Identity Taxation in the Academy," *Gender and Education* 24, no. 2 (January 2012): 213–27. https://doi.org/10.1080/09540253.2011.606208.
6. Benjamin Baez, "Race-Related Service and Faculty of Color: Conceptualizing Critical Agency in Academe," *Higher Education* 39 (April 2000): 363–91. https://doi.org/10.1023/a:1003972214943.
7. Joya Misra, Alexandra Kuvaeva, KerryAnn O'Meara, Dawn Kiyoe Culpepper, and Audrey Jaeger, "Gendered and Racialized Perceptions of Faculty Workloads," *Gender & Society* 35, no. 3 (April 14, 2021): 358–94. https://doi.org/10.1177/08912432211001387.

Chapter 28

The Importance of Having Female College Presidents in the Ivy League

FELECIA COMMODORE, *University of Illinois, Urbana-Champaign*

WHILE WOMEN MAKE UP ABOUT 60% of undergraduate as well as master's and doctoral students in the United States, a far lower percentage of the presidents of American colleges and universities are women. The Ivy League has been select-ing female presidents for a few decades. Judith Rodin was the first, in 1994, when she became the president of the University of Pennsylvania. She was followed by Ruth Simmons at Brown University and Shirley Tilghman at Princeton Univer-sity, both in 2001. Rodin was succeeded by another woman, Amy Guttman, in 2004.

Ivy League institutions are often seen as exemplars of elite, complex institutions. So seeing female leaders in the Ivy League could signal the benefit of women in leadership to other governing boards that are hesitant or slow to hire women as presidents.

How Uncommon Are Female Presidents across Higher Ed?

Despite what may seem like a boom in women leading institutions, the percentage of women in the presidency at colleges and universities more broadly has plateaued at 25% to 30% for the past decade. This was after increasing from 9.5% in 1986 to 19% in 1998.

A number of factors contribute to this low percentage, including barriers within the college presidential pipeline—such as exclusion from networks that provide mentorship—reward and promotion structures that are not equitable across genders and bias against women in academic leadership roles.[1] A recent analysis of data on college presidents explains how this bias against women occurs when it comes to academic leadership roles.[2] This is important because college presidents typically find their way to the presidency through academic leadership roles such as dean, vice provost, and provost.

I think it would be more surprising to see mostly female presidents at large public research universities, or at a majority of the schools in the Power 5 athletic conferences, than at Ivy League institutions.

What Are the Priorities of College Presidents?

The biggest priority depends on the individual college or university. All institutions, however, must ensure they are financially healthy and identify opportunities to strengthen their financial resources. College presidents have reported that they spend the most time on budget and financial management, followed by fund-raising.

In the current higher education marketplace, where the average cost of college runs over US$35,000 per year, college leaders must work to keep their institutions fiscally strong and also competitive and affordable. This may involve, for example, building new infrastructure,[3] creating new programs, and cultivating new sources of funding.

What Effect Does Having a Woman in the Top Seat Have?

For colleges that have only ever had a man in the president's role, hiring their first woman as president can signal that the institution embraces change and evolution. This can be an especially important message to send to funders, alumni donors, philanthropists, state legislators, and corporate partners, who all play a role in ensuring a college's financial vitality.

Female presidents add to the diversity of the college presidency. They add different perspectives to conversations that shape practices and policies both within their college and across higher education. They might, for example, provide their own perspective on compensation for female faculty members of color, who tend to engage in more unpaid service work on campuses.[4] Organizational scholars and business leaders affirm that diversity strengthens the decisions made by organizations and contributes to innovative solutions.[5] A more diverse group of decision makers can generate more decision alternatives than a homogeneous group that may be susceptible to group-think.

Lastly, having women at the helm of academic institutions shows other women who aspire to become college presidents that it is indeed possible.[6]

Notes

1. Victoria L. Brescoll, "Leading with Their Hearts? How Gender Stereotypes of Emotion Lead to Biased Evaluations of Female Leaders," *Leadership Quarterly* 27, no. 3 (June 2016): 415–28. https://doi.org/10.1016/j.leaqua.2016.02.005.
2. Hanna Rodriguez-Farrar and L. Hazel Jack, "An Unrecognized Bias Contributing to the Gender Gap in the College Presidency," Higher Education Today blog, March 6, 2023. https://www.higheredtoday.org/2023/03/06/an-unrecognized-bias-contributing-to-the-gender-gap-in-the-college-presidency/.
3. Kevin R. McClure, "Building the Innovative and Entrepreneurial University: An Institutional Case Study of Administrative Academic Capitalism." *Journal of Higher Education* 87, no. 4 (2016): 516–43. https://doi.org/10.1080/00221546.2016.11777412.
4. Laura E. Hirshfield and Tiffany D. Joseph, "'We Need a Woman, We Need a Black Woman': Gender, Race, and Identity Taxation in the Academy," *Gender and Education* 24, no. 2 (2012): 213–27. https://doi.org/10.1080/09540253.2011.606208.
5. Kathyayini Rao and Carol Tilt, "Board Composition and Corporate Social Responsibility: The Role of Diversity, Gender, Strategy and Decision Making," *Journal of Business Ethics* 138 (March 17, 2015): 327–47. https://doi.org/10.1007/s10551-015-2613-5; Yang Yang and Alison M. Konrad, "Diversity and Organizational Innovation: The Role of Employee Involvement," *Journal of Organizational Behavior* 32, no. 8 (November 2011): 1062–83. https://doi.org/10.1002/job.724.
6. Lilian H. Hill and Celeste A. Wheat, "The Influence of Mentorship and Role Models on University Women Leaders' Career Paths to University Presidency," *Qualitative Report* 22, no. 8 (August 7, 2017): 2090–111. https://doi.org/10.46743/2160-3715/2017.2437.

Part VI.

Academic Life Is Getting More Difficult

Along with the challenges of implementing diversity and equity initiatives in a shifting political landscape, academic life for faculty is getting more difficult. The increasing political polarization within our country, the use of artificial intelligence (AI) in teaching and learning, worker shortages in crucial areas like health care and PK–12 education, and attacks on tenure and academic freedom all combine to create a more difficult work environment for faculty. The chapters in part VI give details on these challenges, often from front-line faculty doing the work.

Rising mental health issues among college students and faculty pose additional challenges for faculty and make prioritizing faculty well-being even more of an urgent issue for campus leaders. As Coleman highlights, there is an alarming increase in mental health problems among college students, and the faculty and staff who support them are struggling to keep up with these problems. While the challenges of recovering from social isolation during the COVID-19 pandemic account for part of what universities are facing, they are also dealing with an increasingly chaotic everyday reality filled with wars, climate crises, and rising fascism and other threats to democracy. While much attention has been paid to student mental health, faculty burnout is also on the rise, and part of faculty self-care requires figuring out how to set boundaries with students.

AI is one of the most contested and polarizing topics on college campuses today. This technology is both a boon and a source of concern in academic circles. As AI continues to reshape teaching and learning, educators and institutions must grapple with its multifaceted implications, including concerns of academic integrity and the changing role of professors. AI is not only a challenge to ways of learning, but it is also a challenge to the traditional role of the professoriate, with Young predicting a future where their traditional role is radically redefined by AI.

Amid these challenges, Letourneau shows us that faculty shortages in vital fields such as health care and education are also occurring. The consequences of these shortages extend beyond campuses, impacting the workforce in critical sectors and, by extension, society.

On top of these shortages, academic tenure, a cornerstone of faculty job security, is under threat, and, as Justice points out, tenure rates have declined, and the use of non-tenure-track faculty on campuses has increased. Academic tenure has traditionally been a safeguard of faculty job security and academic freedom. The decline of tenure and the silencing of faculty can have long-term detrimental impacts on student protest and freedom of speech, not just on our campuses today but also on our democracy in the future.

Chapter 29

5 Ways College Instructors Can Help Students Take Care of Their Mental Health

MAX COLEMAN, *University of Utah*

A FEW YEARS AGO, a student showed up in my class looking distraught. "I don't think I can be in class today," the student told me. No explanation, no elaboration.

I knew from our previous conversations that this student suffered from anxiety and that the previous few weeks had been overwhelming for her. I allowed the student to leave class. When I checked in with her later that day, she said she was feeling a lot better but was just stressed because of everything on her plate.

That conversation took place in 2016. Rates of mental health problems had already been on the rise. From 2012 to 2018, for example, the number of self-reported suicide attempts more than doubled among college undergraduates.[1]

Since then—in large part because of the COVID-19 pandemic—college leaders have expressed increased concern for the mental health of students. In September 2020, 61% of college presidents at four-year public institutions identified the mental health of students as a top concern. A year later, that figure jumped to 71%.[2]

As a researcher studying the sociology of mental health, I have long been worried about the high rates of mental illness and general distress among college students. Based on my review of recent scholarship on these issues—along with guidance from mental health practitioners who work in a college setting—I developed a set of best practices for instructors and others who wish to see college students flourish.[3] Here are five practices that emerged from my research.

1. Signal Support in the Syllabus and in Class

The syllabus is one of the first opportunities that instructors have to demonstrate their openness and commitment to students' mental health. Though many universities now require instructors to describe campus resources and accommodations available to students with disabilities, it may also be helpful to include additional language on mental health.

At the very least, instructors can provide information about the student counseling center, including the location, contact information, and number of free appointments, if any.

For students in online classes, the syllabus can specify which counseling services are available off campus and how to access them.

Instructors can also signal their support in the classroom. During challenging periods, such as midterms and finals, instructors can consider saying something along these lines: "I know this is a stressful time. Please reach out if you feel like you're falling behind or if you just want to talk. I want to remind you of the free services available at the student counseling center." Such statements not only show empathy, but they also steer students toward essential resources.

2. Identify At-risk Students

A study by the Boston University School of Public Health found that 71% of faculty would appreciate some kind of checklist to help them identify students in emotional distress.[4] While warning signs may differ from one student to the next, a few key indicators to look for are these: a sudden decline in academic performance; repeated absences from class; failure to respond to outreach; and changes in weight, grooming, or personality.

3. Question, Persuade, Refer

For instructors who encounter a student in psychological distress, consider using the well-established QPR protocol: question, persuade, refer. While not developed for a college population, QPR has been shown to be effective in a college setting, leading to "increases in suicide prevention knowledge, attitudes and skills."[5] Even when students' mental health concerns do not present a suicide risk, instructors can draw on the QPR protocol or a related approach, such as the validate-appreciate-refer approach of the nonprofit Active Minds.

Instructors can implement the QPR protocol as follows: Question the student by gently raising your concerns after class, during office hours, or via email. Professor David Gooblar of the University of Iowa, when sharing advice he learned from the school's director of counseling services, suggests, "You can say, hey, you seem a little off these days. Is everything OK?"[6] If the student says that things are not going well, persuade the student to seek treatment, and refer the student to the college counseling center. If you fear your student may be suicidal, ask directly, "Are you thinking about killing yourself?" Many people believe that asking this question will exacerbate suicidal thoughts, but this is a myth.[7] Instead, it can help at-risk students get the help they need.

Instructors can ask their campus's counseling center if there are opportunities to receive formal training, such as ASIST, which is short for applied suicide intervention skills training.

4. Address Real-World Issues and Events

Students don't live in a vacuum. Events such as the murder of George Floyd and the rise in hate crimes against Asian Americans have been linked to mental health challenges among Black students[8] and Asian American or Pacific Islander students,[9] respectively. As Active Minds recommends, give students a chance to share their thoughts whenever "a major event has happened on campus, in the community, or nationally that you suspect may be on the students' minds."[10]

5. Don't Forget about Your Own Mental Health

More than one in five faculty members indicated in a 2021 survey that caring for students' mental health was taxing their own.[11] Instructor burnout is a serious concern that requires an institutional response. In the meantime, self-care may require setting boundaries with students to protect one's own well-being. Instructors can also take advantage of existing campus resources, such as their employee assistance program.

While instructors and community members rally university leaders to devote more resources to mental health, college instructors would do well to prepare for times when a student reaches out to express thoughts of suicide, shows signs of major depression, or mentions the trauma of sexual assault. Instructors can also take proactive steps to address mental health more broadly, including by directing students to the resources they need before such challenges arise.

Notes

1. Mary E. Duffy, Jean M. Twenge, and Thomas E. Joiner, "Trends in Mood and Anxiety Symptoms and Suicide-Related Outcomes among U.S. Undergraduates, 2007–2018: Evidence from Two National Surveys," *Journal of Adolescent Health* 65, no. 5 (July 3, 2019): 590–98. https://doi.org/10.1016/j.jadohealth.2019.04.033.
2. Danielle Melidona, Morgan Taylor, and Ty C. McNamee, "2021 Fall Term Pulse Point Survey of College and University Presidents," American Council on Education, October 25, 2021. https://www.acenet.edu/Research-Insights/Pages/Senior-Leaders/Presidents-Survey-Fall-2021.aspx.
3. Max E. Coleman, "Mental Health in the College Classroom: Best Practices for Instructors," *Teaching Sociology* 50, no. 2 (February 25, 2022): 168–82. https://doi.org/10.1177/0092055x221080433.
4. *The Role of Faculty in Student Mental Health*, Boston University and the Mary Christie Foundation, https://marychristieinstitute.org/wp

    -content/uploads/2021/04/The-Role-of-Faculty-in-Student-Mental
    -Health.pdf.

5. Sharon L. Mitchell, Mahrin Kader, Sherri A. Darrow, Melinda Z.
    Haggerty, and Niki L. Keating, "Evaluating Question, Persuade, Refer
    (QPR) Suicide Prevention Training in a College Setting," *Journal of
    College Student Psychotherapy* 27, no. 2 (April 3, 2013): 138–48.
    https://doi.org/10.1080/87568225.2013.766109.

6. David Gooblar, "How to Help a Student in a Mental-Health Crisis,"
    Chronicle of Higher Education, December 17, 2018. https://www
    .chronicle.com/article/how-to-help-a-student-in-a-mental-health
    -crisis.

7. T. Dazzi, R. Gribble, S. Wessely, and N. T. Fear, "Does Asking about
    Suicide and Related Behaviours Induce Suicidal Ideation? What Is the
    Evidence?," *Psychological Medicine* 44, no. 16 (July 7, 2014): 3361–63.
    https://doi.org/10.1017/s0033291714001299.

8. Laura C. L. Landertinger, Elijah Greene, Miracle Cooper, and Anita
    Hopson, "Emotional and Mental Health Support for Black Students:
    Responding to Racial Trauma and White Terror amidst COVID-19,"
    Journal of Higher Education Management 36, no. 1 (April 2021):
    154–64.

9. Sasha Zhou, Rachel Banawa, and Hans Oh, "Stop Asian Hate: The
    Mental Health Impact of Racial Discrimination among Asian Pacific
    Islander Young and Emerging Adults during COVID-19," *Health
    Services Research* 56, no. S2 (September 15, 2021): 8–9. https://doi
    .org/10.1111/1475-6773.13723.

10. *Creating a Culture of Caring*, a faculty resource, Active Minds,
    https://www.activeminds.org/wp-content/uploads/2020/04/Faculty
    -Resource_Creating-a-Culture-of-Caring.pdf.

11. *Role of Faculty in Student Mental Health*, Boston University and the
    Mary Christie Foundation.

Chapter 30

Should Artificial Intelligence Be Permitted in College Classrooms?
4 Scholars Weigh In

NICHOLAS TAMPIO, *Fordham University*

PATRICIA A. YOUNG, *University of Maryland, Baltimore County*

ASIM ALI, *Auburn University*

SHITAL THEKDI, *University of Richmond*

ONE OF THE MOST INTENSE discussions taking place among university faculty today is whether to permit students to use artificial intelligence in their coursework. Four scholars offer their takes on AI as a learning tool and explain the reasons why they will or won't be making it a part of their classes.

Learn to Think for Yourself. By Nicholas Tampio

As a professor, I believe the purpose of a college class is to teach students to think: to read scholarship, ask questions, formulate a thesis, collect and analyze data, draft an essay, take feedback from the instructor and other students, and write a final draft.[1] One problem with ChatGPT is that it allows students to produce a decent paper without thinking or writing for themselves.

In my class on American political thought, I assign speeches by Martin Luther King Jr. and Malcolm X and ask students to compose an essay on what King and X might say about a current American political debate, such as a judicial decision on affirmative action. Students could get fine grades if they used ChatGPT to "write" their papers. But they will have missed a chance to enter a dialogue with two profound thinkers about a topic that could reshape American higher education and society.

The point of learning to write is not simply intellectual self-discovery. My students go on to careers in journalism, law, science, academia, and business. Their employers will ask them to research and write about a topic. Few employers will likely hire someone to use a large language model that relies on an algorithm to scrape databases filled with errors and biases. Already, a lawyer has gotten in trouble for using ChatGPT to craft a motion filled with fabricated cases.[2] Employees succeed when they themselves can research a topic and write intelligently about it.

Artificial intelligence is a tool that defeats a purpose of a college education—to learn how to think, and write, for oneself.

ChatGPT Doesn't Promote Advanced Thinking.
By Patricia A. Young

College students who are operating from a convenience or entitlement mentality—one in which they think, "I am entitled to use whatever technology is available to me"—will naturally gravitate toward using ChatGPT with or without their professor's permission. Using ChatGPT and submitting a course assignment as one's own creation is called AI-assisted plagiarism.[3]

Some professors allow the use of ChatGPT as long as students cite it as the source. As a researcher who specializes in the use of technology in education, I believe this practice needs to be thought through. Does this mean that ChatGPT would need to cite its sources so that students could cite ChatGPT as a type of secondary source according to the reference style of the American Psychological Association, a standard citation style? What Pandora's box are we opening? Some users report that ChatGPT never reveals its sources anyway.

The proliferation of free AI means that students won't have to think much while writing—just engage in a high level of copy and paste. We used to call that plagiarism. AI-assisted plagiarism has the potential for ushering in a new era of academic misconduct.

The consequences will come when students take higher-level courses or land a job and lack the literacy skills to perform competently. We will have created a generation of functionally illiterate adults who lack the capacity to engage in advanced thinking—like critiquing or comparing and contrasting information.

Yes, students can and should use smart tools, but we need to hypothesize and measure the costs to human ingenuity and the future of the human race.

AI Is Another Teacher. By Asim Ali

I teach information systems management, and in the spring of 2023, I had students use ChatGPT for an assignment and then record a video podcast discussing how AI will impact their careers. In subsequent terms, I am being more intentional by providing guidance on the possibilities and limitations of AI tools for each assignment. For example, students learn that using generative AI on a self-reflection assignment may not help, but using AI to analyze a case study is potentially a great way to augment their own insights. This emulates their future jobs in which they may use AI tools to enhance the quality of their work product.

My experience with adapting to AI for my own course inspired me to create a resource for all my colleagues. As the executive director of the Biggio Center for the Enhancement of Teaching and Learning, I oversee the instructional design and educational development teams at Auburn University. We created a self-paced online course called Teaching with AI. As of 2024, there were over 700 faculty at Auburn and thousands other faculty at over 80 institutions who were engaging with the content and with one another through discussion boards and practical exercises.

I receive messages from faculty who share ways they are changing their assignments or discussing AI with their students. Some see AI as a threat to humans, but my discussing AI with students and with colleagues across the country has helped me develop human connections.

What Can You Do That AI Can't? By Shital Thekdi

This semester I will ask students taking my course Statistics for Business and Economics to discuss the question "What is your value beyond AI tools?" I want them to reframe the conversation on AI from one of academic integrity into one about AI's challenge for them instead. I believe students must recognize that the jobs they imagine will exist for them could be eliminated because of these new technologies. So the pressure is on students to understand not only how to use these tools but also how to be better than the tools.

I hope my students will consider ethical reasoning and the role of human connections. While AI can be trained to make value-based decisions, individuals and groups have their own values that can differ considerably from those used by AI. And AI tools do not have the capacity to form human connections and experiences.

I believe it's our responsibility as educators to prepare our students for a rapidly evolving cultural and technological landscape.

Notes

1. Nicholas Tampio, *Teaching Political Theory: A Pluralistic Approach* (Cheltenham, UK: Edward Elgar, 2022).
2. Matt Novak, "Lawyer Uses ChatGPT in Federal Court and It Goes Horribly Wrong," *Forbes*, May 27, 2023. https://www.forbes.com/sites/mattnovak/2023/05/27/lawyer-uses-chatgpt-in-federal-court-and-it-goes-horribly-wrong/?sh=7d65ded43494.
3. Yunkai Xiao, Soumyadeep Chatterjee, and Edward Gehringer, "A New Era of Plagiarism: The Danger of Cheating Using AI" (conference paper, 20th International Conference on Information Technology Based Higher Education and Training, Antalya, Turkey, 2022). https://doi.org/10.1109/ithet56107.2022.10031827.

The Future of College Will Involve Fewer Professors

PATRICIA A. YOUNG, *University of Maryland, Baltimore County*

AT A LARGE PRIVATE UNIVERSITY in Northern California, a business professor uses an avatar to lecture on a virtual stage. Meanwhile, at a southern university, graduate students in an artificial intelligence course discover that one of their nine teaching assistants is a virtual avatar, Jill Watson, also known as Watson, IBM's question-answering computer system. Of the 10,000 messages posted to an online message board in one semester, Jill participated in student conversations and responded to all inquiries with 97% accuracy. At a private college on the East Coast, students

Some colleges and universities will use
AI technology to help teach their students,
which may bring changes to traditional
classrooms.
skynesher / E+ via Getty Images

interact with an AI chat agent in a virtual restaurant set in
China to learn the Mandarin language.

These examples provide a glimpse into the future
of teaching and learning in college. It is a future that will
involve a drastically reduced role for full-time tenured or
tenure-track faculty who teach face-to-face. I forecast
this future scenario and others in a 2021 book.[1] As a researcher who specializes in educational technology, I see
three trends that will shrink the role of traditional college
professors.

1. The Rise of Artificial Intelligence

According to a 2021 Educause poll on AI, many institutions
of higher education find themselves more focused on the

present limited use of AI—for tasks such as detecting plagiarism or proctoring—and not so much on the future of AI.[2] AI's use in higher education has largely been concerned with digital assistants and chat agents.[3] These technologies focus on the teaching and learning of students.

In my view, universities should broaden their use of AI and conduct experiments to improve upon its usefulness to individual learners. For example, how can colleges use AI to improve student learning of calculus or help students become stronger writers?

Most universities are slow to innovate, however. According to the same Educause poll, some of the challenges to acquiring and using AI included a lack of technical expertise, financial concerns, insufficient leadership, and biased algorithms.

Rensselaer Polytechnic Institute and the Massachusetts Institute of Technology are leading the way with new uses of AI. In an immersion lab staged as a food market in China, Rensselaer virtually transports students learning Mandarin Chinese into this market to interact with AI avatars. MIT has devoted millions of dollars to faculty research in AI. One of MIT's projects—called RAISE, for Responsible AI for Social Empowerment and Education—will support how people from diverse backgrounds learn with AI.

Professors from the baby-boom generation are retiring, and I expect some of their jobs will not be filled. In many cases, these coveted positions will be replaced by part-time and temporary faculty. I believe the rising use of AI will contribute to this trend, with universities relying more on technology and less on in-person teaching.

2. Erosion of Academic Tenure

Tenure is a status that grants professors protections against being fired without due cause or under extraordinary circumstances.

The COVID-19 pandemic became a reason to override and diminish the power of shared leadership with faculty. That included voiding faculty handbooks, regulations, and employment contracts. The Kansas Board of Regents in January 2021 voted to allow emergency terminations and suspensions—including for tenured faculty—to alleviate fiscal pressures placed on state universities by the pandemic. Ultimately, the pandemic was an opportunity for universities to downsize unproductive faculty and keep "active practitioners."

Long before the pandemic there had been a decline over time in the number of tenured faculty positions. According to the American Association of University Professors, the proportion of part-time and full-time non-tenure-track faculty grew from 55% in 1975 to 70% in 2015. Conversely, the proportion of full-time tenured and tenure-track faculty fell from 45% to 30% over that same period.[4]

3. The Flipped Classroom

The flipped classroom provides students with opportunities to view, listen, and learn at their own pace through video instruction outside the classroom. It has been around since at least 2007.

This teaching approach is similar to the way people learn from one another by watching videos on YouTube or TikTok. In college the flipped classroom involves pre-recorded faculty lectures on course content, which might be on the causes of the US Civil War or on the origin of white rice. In class, students build on the professor's pre-recorded lecture and work on activities to advance discussion and expand knowledge. The classroom becomes a place for social interaction and understanding course content. The flipped classroom maximizes instructional time for the professor and students because the lecture comes before the course's in-class session.

When a professor records a video on a subject area, this same video can be viewed by one student or thousands of students. A human teaching assistant, avatar, or chat agent could conduct all in-class activities, tests, and group work. No additional professors would be needed to teach multiple sections of the same course. Professors, in this scenario, serve a limited role and ultimately will be needed less.

These three trends mean that the professoriate, as I see it, is on the cusp of a radical transformation.

Notes

1. Patricia A. Young, *Human Specialization in Design and Technology: The Current Wave for Learning, Culture, Industry, and Beyond* (Abingdon, UK: Routledge, 2020).
2. *2021 EDUCAUSE Horizon Report: Teaching and Learning Edition*, EDUCAUSE, April 26, 2021. https://library.educause.edu/resources /2021/4/2021-educause-horizon-report-teaching-and-learning -edition.
3. D. Christopher Brooks, "EDUCAUSE QuickPoll Results: Artificial Intelligence Use in Higher Education," EDUCAUSE, June 11, 2011. https://er.educause.edu/articles/2021/6/educause-quickpoll-results -artificial-intelligence-use-in-higher-education.
4. "Trends in the Academic Labor Force, 1975–2015," bar graph, American Association of University Professors Research Office, March 2017. https://www.aaup.org/sites/default/files/Academic_Labor_Force _Trends_1975-2015.pdf.

Chapter 32

The US Doesn't Have Enough Faculty to Train the Next Generation of Nurses

RAYNA M. LETOURNEAU, *University of South Florida*

DESPITE A NATIONAL NURSING SHORTAGE in the United States, over 91,000 qualified applications were not accepted at US nursing schools in 2021, according to the American Association of Colleges of Nursing.[1] This was due primarily to a shortage of nursing professors and a limited number of clinical placements where nursing students get practical job training. Additional constraints include a shortage of experienced practitioners to provide supervision during clinical training, insufficient classroom space, and inadequate financial resources. Although the 91,000 may not account for students who apply to multiple nursing schools, it clearly suggests that not all qualified students are able to enroll in nursing school.

I am a nurse researcher, professor of nursing, and executive director of the Florida Center for Nursing, the state's nursing workforce center. I've found that the nursing shortage is a complex issue that involves many factors—but chief among them is the shortage of faculty to train future nurses.

Growing Demand for Nurses

There are not enough new nurses entering the US health care system each year to meet the country's growing demand. This can have serious consequences for patient safety and quality of care.[2]

Nationally, the number of jobs for registered nurses is projected to increase by 6% between 2022 and 2032. Some states project an even higher demand for registered nurses because of their population and their needs. In 2024, the US Bureau of Labor Statistics estimated there will be about 193,100 openings for registered nurses each year over the next decade to meet the demands of the growing population and also to replace nurses who retire or quit the profession.[3] This means the United States will need about two million new registered nurses by 2034.

In addition to a shortage of registered nurses, there is also a shortage of nurse practitioners. The category of nurse practitioner is projected to be the second-fastest-growing occupation in the next decade, after wind-turbine technicians, with a projected increase of 52.2%. Nurse practitioners have an advanced scope of practice compared with registered nurses. They must complete additional clinical hours, earn a master's or doctoral degree in nursing, and complete additional certifications to work with specific patient populations.

The COVID-19 pandemic exacerbated the health and wellness problems of the nursing workforce. Despite these problems, student enrollment in nursing schools increased in 2020. The pandemic has not turned people away from wanting to pursue a career in nursing. However, without enough nursing faculty and clinical sites, there will not be enough new nurses to meet the health care demands of the nation.

Need for More Nursing Faculty

In 2022, the national nurse faculty vacancy rate was 8.8%, an increase from the 2020 rate of 6.5%. More than half of all nursing schools report vacant full-time faculty positions. The highest need is in nursing programs in western and southern states.

Nursing education in clinical settings requires smaller student-to-faculty ratios than do many other professions in order to maintain the safety of patients, students, and faculty members. Regulatory agencies recommend at least 1 faculty member to no more than 10 students engaged in clinical learning.

The faculty shortage is also affected by the fact that many current nursing faculty members are reaching retirement age. The percentage of full-time nursing faculty members aged 60 and older increased from roughly 18% in 2006 to nearly 31% in 2015.[4] The American Association of Colleges of Nursing reports that the average ages of doctorate-educated nursing faculty at the ranks of professor, associate professor, and assistant professor were 62.5 years, 56.7 years, and 50.6 years, respectively.[5]

Another factor that contributes to the nursing faculty shortage, and the most critical issue related to faculty recruitment, is compensation. The salary of a nurse with an advanced degree is much higher in clinical and private sectors than it is in academia.

According to a survey by the American Association of Nurse Practitioners, the median salary of a nurse practitioner, across settings and specialties, is $110,000. By contrast, the American Association of Colleges of Nursing reported in March 2022 that the average salary for master's-prepared professors in nursing schools was just under $90,000.

Fixing the Faculty Shortage

Innovative strategies are needed to address the nursing faculty shortage. The Title VIII Nursing Workforce Reauthorization Act of 2019 was a start. The act provides funding for nursing faculty development, for scholarships, and for loan repayment for nurses, as well as grants for advanced nursing education, nursing diversity initiatives, and other priorities.

In addition to national strategies, individual states are addressing the shortage at the local level. Maryland, for example, awarded over US$29 million in grants to 14 higher education institutions with nursing programs in Maryland to increase the number of qualified nurses.

Finally, offering faculty salaries comparable to those in clinical settings may attract more nurses to use their expertise to train and expand the next generation of health care workers.

Notes

1. Robert Rosseter, "Nursing Faculty Shortage Fact Sheet," American Association of Colleges of Nursing, 2022. https://www.aacnnursing .org/Portals/0/PDFs/Fact-Sheets/Faculty-Shortage-Factsheet.pdf.
2. Benjamin U. Friedrich and Martin B. Hackmann, "The Returns to Nursing: Evidence from a Parental-Leave Program," *Review of Economic Studies* 88, no. 5 (January 28, 2021): 2308–43. https://doi.org/10.1093/restud /rdaa082.
3. "Registered Nurses," Occupational Outlook Handbook, US Department of Labor, Bureau of Labor Statistics, accessed June 1, 2024. https://www.bls.gov/ooh/healthcare/registered-nurses.htm.
4. Di Fang and Karen Kesten, "Retirements and Succession of Nursing Faculty in 2016–2025." *Nursing Outlook* 65, no. 5 (September 2017): 633–42. https://doi.org/10.1016/j.outlook.2017.03.003.
5. Rosseter, "Fact Sheet: Faculty Nursing Shortage."

Chapter 33

Academic Tenure
What It Is and Why It Matters

GEORGE JUSTICE, *University of Tulsa*

OF ALL THE THINGS THAT UNIVERSITY professors can achieve in their career, few are as desirable as academic tenure. A subject of contemporary controversy, tenure continues to exist in American higher education. A survey of provosts—the chief academic officers of higher education institutions—found that they supported retaining the tenure system on their campuses.[1] A provost myself and the author of *How to Be a Dean*,[2] I discuss the origin of tenure and the waning protections it affords today to the decreasing percentage of professors at US colleges and universities who have it.

What Is Academic Tenure?

Academic tenure is a system of strong job protections that virtually guarantees a university professor will never be fired or let go except in extreme of circumstances. A key idea behind tenure is to allow faculty to speak freely—whether on campus or in public—without fear of reprisal.

Achieving tenure is not easy or quick to do.

An aspiring tenured professor must secure a "tenure track" position after graduating from a PhD program, followed in many cases by one or more postdoctoral fellowships prior to landing a tenure-track job as an assistant professor. Then, in a probationary period, which can last from 5 to 10 years but typically takes 7, the assistant professor must demonstrate academic excellence in teaching, research, and service to the campus community. The probationary period is then followed by a yearlong process during which the professor's work is evaluated by peer faculty—both inside and outside the university where the professor teaches—as well as by administrators at the institution.

If assistant professors succeed in getting tenure, they can be promoted to the rank of associate professor. But if they are denied tenure, it usually means they have one more year to build up their credentials and find employment at another college or university—or else leave academia altogether to find work in a different industry.

A little less than half of all full-time faculty at colleges and universities in the United States—45.1%, or 375,286, according to 2019 data—have tenure.[3] That number declined to 44.8% in 2021, according to the National Center for Education Statistics.

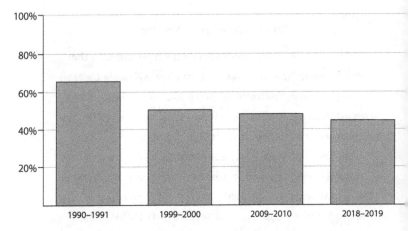

The percentage of tenured professors fell over time in the United States. In the 1990–91 academic year, 65.2% of professors at four-year colleges held academic tenure, but data from 2018–19 shows that the number had dwindled down to just under half.

The Conversation, CC-BY-ND. National Center for Education Statistics

When Did Tenure First Appear?

The tenure system was created in the early twentieth century as a partnership between faculty and the institutions that employed them. Faculty came to be represented nationally by the American Association of University Professors, which was founded in 1915 by two of the era's most famous intellectuals: John Dewey and Arthur O. Lovejoy. The association wasn't a union, although now it does help faculty unionize.

In 1940, the association teamed up with the Association of American Colleges—now the Association of American Colleges and Universities—to define tenure as a system providing "an indefinite appointment that can be terminated only for cause or under extraordinary circumstances such as financial exigency and program discontinuation."

The real origin of the concept, though, lay in the practice of nineteenth-century German universities. Faculty in these universities created wide autonomy for their work on the basis of their pursuit of knowledge for its own sake.[4] The greatest freedom and power went to those professors at the top of a rigid hierarchy.

In its 1915 "Declaration of Principles," the American Association of University Professors viewed faculty tenure as a property right and academic freedom as "essential to civilization." Academic freedom includes rights both within and outside a professor's daily work: "freedom of inquiry and research; freedom of teaching within the university or college; and freedom of extramural utterance and action." The last of these freedoms means that faculty can speak up on matters of public concern outside their specialized expertise without fear of losing their job.[5]

Whom Does Tenure Benefit?

As a job protection, tenure directly benefits college teachers. Indirectly, tenure benefits a society that thrives through the education and research that colleges and universities create.

The job protections are significant. Except in extreme circumstances, faculty who have achieved tenure can expect to be paid for teaching and research for as long as they hold their job. There is no retirement age, and colleges only rarely go out of business.

Tenure's benefits have weakened in recent years. Financially battered by COVID-19, institutions let tenured faculty go merely with general assertions of financial stress rather than a deep crisis of "financial exigency."

Termination "with cause" has evolved in recent years. For instance, federal law, including Title IX of the Federal Education Act, has pushed institutions to fire or force the resignation of faculty members who violated core principles of equal treatment, especially through sexual harassment of students.

Why Is Tenure Controversial?

There are economic, political, ideological, and social reasons why tenure has come under fire over the past 50 years.

From an economic perspective, higher education is big business with a big impact on the US economy. State universities are among the biggest businesses in their locale. Some legislators believe that universities should be treated like businesses. Professors would have no more job security than any other employees and could be fired without a rigorous process led by their faculty peers.

"What happens in our private sector should be applied to our universities as well," argued Iowa state senator Bradley Zaun, who introduced legislation that would have eliminated tenure in his state's public universities.[6] The measure failed.

In socially conservative parts of the country, legislators allege that professors have hypocritically violated students' freedom of speech, such as by interfering with their participation in conservative student political groups.

Actions against tenured faculty originate not just with social conservatives. Colleges have suspended faculty members for using racial slurs that offended students. The recent conflict in the Middle East has changed the political nature of challenges to tenured faculty members' activism. For example, Indiana University professor Abdulkader Sinno was suspended in early 2024 for reserving a room for a student group advocating for Palestinians.

What Is Tenure's Future?

Academic leaders have hired increasing numbers of less expensive faculty without tenure or not on the tenure track over the past few decades. The percentage of tenured college teachers has fallen to 44.8% in 2022 from nearly 65% in 1980. Recent analysis suggests that if part-time faculty are included, a mere quarter of college teachers have tenure.

While research shows that diverse faculty and peer viewpoints lead to a richer education for students, the tenured faculty are whiter and more male than the general body of college teachers, let alone the US population. Indeed, tenured faculty have become demographically inconsistent with the students in their classrooms: 73% of college professors are white, whereas 51.1% of the population under 24 years old was non-Hispanic white in 2019.[7]

Is the practice of academic freedom "essential to civilization"? Does it require tenure for faculty? Or is tenure a destructive job perk that limits innovation in an important service industry by entrenching faculty who may be mediocre and old-fashioned in their teaching and research? The one thing guaranteed in the future of tenure is that as long as it exists, it will continue to be controversial.

Notes

1. *Inside Higher Ed: 2021 Survey of College and University Chief Academic Officers*, a research report from *Inside Higher Ed* and Hanover Research (Hoboken, NJ: Wiley, 2021).
2. George Justice, *How to Be a Dean* (Baltimore: Johns Hopkins University Press, 2019).

3. Table 316.81: Percentage of full-time faculty (instruction, research, and public service) with tenure at degree-granting postsecondary institutions with a tenure system, by control, level, and state: 2018–19, Institute for Education Sciences, National Center for Education Statistics. https://nces.ed.gov/programs/digest/d19/tables/dt19_316.81.asp.

4. Lenore O'Boyle, "Learning for Its Own Sake: The German University as Nineteenth-Century Model," *Comparative Studies in Society and History* 25, no. 1 (January 1983): 3–25. https://doi.org/10.1017/s0010417500010288.

5. "1915 Declaration of Principles on Academic Freedom and Academic Tenure," archived by the American Association of University Professors. https://www.aaup.org/NR/rdonlyres/A6520A9D-0A9A-47B3-B550-C006B5B224E7/0/1915Declaration.pdf.

6. Kat Mouawad, "Iowa Senator Wants to End Tenure at State Universities," College Fix, February 11, 2021. https://www.thecollegefix.com/iowa-senator-wants-to-end-tenure-at-state-public-universities/.

7. "Fast Facts: Race/Ethnicity of College Faculty," National Center for Education Statistics, 2021. https://nces.ed.gov/fastfacts/display.asp?id=61.

Student Activism and Free Speech on Campus

As I write the introduction to part VII, college campuses across the country and the globe are surging with student activism. At present, the issue is the war in Palestine and Israel. In the past, it was Vietnam, Occupy Wall Street, MeToo, and Black Lives Matter. Freedom of speech and activism have been crucial elements of change in our country's democracy, and student activism and free speech are central aspects of the modern academic reality.

In their idealized imaginings and when they are fulfilling their missions, universities are meant to be forums for critical thinking and the exchange of ideas. While that may be aspirational for many of our institutions, tensions often arise when students assert their voices on contentious topics. The role of higher education in shaping informed and engaged citizens is inextricably linked to this tension. The chapters in part VII highlight the important role that colleges and universities play in fostering free speech and activism.

Conservative media often represents academia as a place where students are brainwashed into a culture of left-wing ideology, yet the piece by Ryan and McNeilly shows that when it comes to free expression, peers have a stronger influence over self-censorship and free expression than college professors. As Vivian points out, the "free speech crisis" that positions universities as a threat to democracy couldn't be farther from the truth. College campuses are one of the only places in the United States where there is still an active fight for freedom of speech.

When we view a college education as a public good and as a necessary component of a thriving democracy and a more just future, we can see that the refrain of "college isn't for everyone" and mainstream media attacks on higher education contribute to the erosion of democracy. In our country, as Conner reminds us, college students are more likely to support free speech and diverse points of view than those who are not in college. At this point in history, we need more tolerance of diversity. While we can admit that democracy is flawed in many ways, I must believe that finding ways to center humanity and live together is what most of us want for the future.

Chapter 34

What Liberals and Conservatives Get Wrong about Free Expression on College Campuses

TIMOTHY J. RYAN, *University of North Carolina, Chapel Hill*

MARK MCNEILLY, *University of North Carolina, Chapel Hill*

WHEN IT COMES TO UNDERSTANDING DISPUTES over free expression on college campuses, such as speakers getting disinvited or having their speeches interrupted, conservatives tend to blame liberal professors for indoctrinating students and ostracizing those who don't agree with liberal viewpoints. One prominent conservative organization, Turning Point USA, has gone so far as to create a database of faculty it says "discriminate against conservative students and advance leftist propaganda in the classroom."[1]

Liberals, in contrast, argue that concerns about free speech on college campuses are overblown. They also accuse conservatives of co-opting the language of free speech proponents in an effort to falsely position themselves as victims.

Our research indicates that both of these narratives are flawed.[2] We are researchers who study political behavior and strategies for business.

We spent a year studying free expression issues at the University of North Carolina at Chapel Hill, a campus that has had a number of flare-ups related to free expression in recent years. We wanted to look beyond single episodes and better understand the typical student's experience concerning free expression. We found that students who identify politically with the Right do indeed face fears of being ostracized that students who identify with the Left do not. However, we also found signs that right-leaning students worry at least as much about reactions from peers as from faculty. Much of this plays out silently in classrooms at Chapel Hill and—we believe—at other colleges and universities throughout the nation.

It's Not about Professors

For our research, we sent surveys to all 20,343 students—the entire undergraduate population at Chapel Hill. Two thousand of these students (randomly selected) were offered an incentive of US$10 to participate in the survey. This feature helped ensure that we heard from a representative cross-section of students. We received 1,087 complete responses.

About half of those respondents were those who got paid for their participation.

For each student who responded, we randomly chose one class from their schedule and asked—for that particular class—how many times during the semester they had kept a sincere opinion related to class to themselves because they were worried about the consequences of expressing it. We found a large liberal/conservative divide: 23% of self-identified liberals said they censored themselves at least once, while 68% of self-identified conservatives did so.

One who hears this finding might presume that behavior by instructors is to blame for this stark difference. But the evidence we gathered does not seem to support this view.

We asked students whether their course instructor "encouraged participation from liberals and conservatives alike." Only 2% of liberal students and 11% of conservatives disagreed with that statement. Similarly, only 6% of liberals and 14% of conservatives disagreed that the same instructor "was interested in learning from people with opinions that differed from the instructor's own opinions." These are low numbers and the splits are small. They are not what one would expect if the claim that liberal instructors try to indoctrinate their students was broadly true.

Fears about Peers

In contrast, students reported substantially more anxiety about how their peers would respond to their expressing sincere political views—and the divides between liberal and conservative students were larger. Seventy-five percent of conservative students said they were concerned that other students would have a lower opinion of them if they expressed their sincere political views in class. Only 26% of liberal students had this concern. Forty-three percent of conservative students were concerned about a negative post on social media. Only 10% of liberal students had this concern.

Pressures that disproportionately affect right-leaning students were evident outside the classroom as well. We asked how often students hear "disrespectful, inappropriate, or offensive comments" about 12 social groups on campus. Students—even those who identified as liberal—acknowledged hearing such comments directed at political conservatives far more often than at any other group.

We also examined whether liberal or conservative students might be more inclined to employ obstructionist tactics, such as blocking the entrance to a public event that featured a speaker with whom they disagree. To do this in an evenhanded way, we presented students with a list of ten political opinions. Then we asked them to choose the opinion that they find most objectionable. We chose a slate of opinions that really exist at UNC, such as ones concerning affirmative action, LGBT rights, and Silent Sam, a Confederate monument that is the subject of a long-running campus controversy

After students chose which opinion they found most objectionable, we asked whether it would be appropriate to take various actions toward people who hold that view. Nearly 20% of liberal respondents indicated it would be appropriate to prevent other students from hearing a campus speaker express the disliked view. But just 3% or less of moderate and conservative respondents indicated that doing so was appropriate.

To understand the typical experience of a university student, we believe it important to go beyond singular dramatic confrontations. The deeper story about free expression on campus, as our study shows, is not just about the shouting that takes place during high-profile incidents on campus. It's also about what students say—and feel compelled to keep to themselves—in lecture halls and classrooms throughout the school year.

Notes

1. Professor Watch List. https://www.professorwatchlist.org/.
2. Timothy J. Ryan, Andrew M. Engelhardt, Jennifer Larson, and Mark McNeilly, "Free Expression and Constructive Dialogue at the University of North Carolina," 2022. https://fecdsurveyreport.web.unc.edu/.

Chapter 35

Saying That Students Embrace Censorship on College Campuses Is Incorrect—Here's How to Discuss the Issue More Constructively

BRADFORD VIVIAN, *Pennsylvania State University*

THE CLAIM THAT COLLEGE STUDENTS censor viewpoints with which they disagree is now common. Versions of this claim include the falsehoods that students "shut down" most invited speakers to campuses, reject challenging ideas, and oppose conservative views.[1] Such cynical distortions dominate discussions of higher education today, misinform the public, and threaten both democracy and higher education. Indeed, politicians in states such as Florida, Texas, and Ohio argue that a so-called "free speech crisis" on college campuses justifies stronger government control over what gets taught in universities.

Since 2020, numerous state legislatures have attempted to censor forms of speech on campuses by citing exaggerations about students and their studies. Passing laws to ban certain kinds of speech or ideas from college campuses is no way to promote true free speech and intellectual diversity. The most common targets of such censorship are programs that discuss race, gender, sexuality, and other forms of multiculturalism.

My concerns over public discourse about higher education extend from my prior work on popular misinformation about universities and why it threatens democracy. I have previously shown that many negative perceptions of students and universities rest on factual distortions and exaggerations.[2]

The character of public debates about higher education is important. Millions of Americans rely on a healthy system of university education for professional and personal success. Rampant cynicism about higher education, leading to decline in public support for it, only undermines their pursuits.

Based on my research, I offer alternative ways to frame debates about higher education. They can lead to discussions that are more constructive and accurate while better protecting fundamental American values such as free speech and democracy.

1. Avoid Stereotypes about College Students

The idea that college students are hostile to opposing viewpoints is false. Pundits and media personalities have promoted this falsehood aggressively. Such figures have benefited, politically or financially, from sensationalism over a so-called free speech crisis on college campuses.

In opinion polls, college students typically express stronger support for free speech and diverse viewpoints than do other groups. Partisan organizations often cherry-pick that data to make it seem otherwise, yet poll results tell only part of the story about college campuses today.

Several thousand institutions make up US higher education. The system includes hundreds of thousands of students from different backgrounds. A college campus is often more demographically and intellectually diverse than its surrounding community. Judgments about higher education based on sweeping generalizations about college students conflict with the full realities of campus life. A wider range of perspectives, including from students themselves, can enrich debates about university education.

2. Consider All Forums for Free Speech in Universities

Universities protect free speech more effectively than do other parts of society. They don't do so perfectly, of course, but more effectively.

Universities are major centers for the study of the First Amendment, the free press, human rights, cultural differences, international diplomacy, and conflict resolution. Many institutions require that students take speech and writing core courses that enhance their skill in argument and debate.

Manufactured outrage about college students who protest invited speakers fuels sensationalism about threatened free speech on campuses. Despite occasional disruptions over bigoted speakers, universities offer numerous forums for free speech, open debate, and intellectual diversity.

One large university holds thousands of classes, meetings, performances, and other events on a daily basis. People freely express their views and pursue new ideas in those settings. Now multiply that reality by several thousand different institutions. Debates over free speech in higher education can be improved by acknowledging the many forums in which people speak freely every day.

3. Recognize the True Threats to Free Speech on Campuses

For the past several years, many state legislatures have promoted the falsehood that universities are hostile to various ideas. The most commonly cited examples are conservative ideas, traditional expressions of patriotism, and great works of Western literature.

The notion of hostility to such ideas on college campuses has surfaced in numerous bills that create new forms of state interference in education. A wave of legislation banning diversity, equity, and inclusion programs in colleges was introduced in numerous state legislatures following the 2020 national election cycle. Many of the proposed bills have been signed into law; many others are pending legislative approval, with still more censorious proposals on the way.

Tenure for faculty members, which protects independent thought, is also under assault in states such as Florida and Texas. Politicians in those states justify ending tenure protections by claiming that professors teach students to censor free speech.

Such rising government interference creates a genuine threat to free speech on college campuses and in society beyond them. A historic increase in state censorship, which began with higher education, has spilled over into censorship of materials about race, gender, sexuality, and multiculturalism in K–12 schools and public libraries.

Advocacy organizations like the American Civil Liberties Union and the American Association of University Professors have condemned this censorship. So have numerous conservative leaders.

Informed scrutiny of university policies and what faculty members teach is always welcome. But cynical distortions have fueled anti-democratic censorship of universities, not constructive efforts to improve them.

4. Understand the Role of Academic Freedom

The ability of citizens to exercise academic freedom is not only vital in education. It's also training for democracy. Academic freedom includes the freedom to attend a university of one's choice; the freedom to learn what one chooses at that university; the freedom of an institution to offer a wide range of subject matter to students; and the freedom to teach or conduct research without political interference.

These freedoms are not reserved for Ivy League universities. US higher education includes state schools and community colleges that serve middle- and working-class students. Those institutions are the main feeder of many professions, from health care and technology to engineering and education.

The quality of public debate over free speech in higher education matters. Government interference with colleges does not punish elites. It rewards deeply cynical views of higher education and restricts a freedom that should be available to all Americans.

Notes

1. "The Growing Partisan Divide in Views of Higher Education," Pew Research Center's Social and Demographic Trends Project, August 19, 2019. https://www.pewresearch.org/social-trends/2019/08/19/the-growing-partisan-divide-in-views-of-higher-education-2/.
2. Bradford Vivian, *Campus Misinformation: The Real Threat to Free Speech in American Higher Education* (New York: Oxford University Press, 2023).

Chapter 36

Not Every Campus Is a Political Battlefield

GRAHAM WRIGHT, *Brandeis University*

LEONARD SAXE, *Brandeis University*

MEDIA REPORTS COMMONLY HIGHLIGHT sensational incidents of political conflicts on American college campuses. But are headlines and anecdotal reports telling the real story?

As scholars of religion and politics, we wanted to get a larger perspective. So between 2015 and 2019, we conducted detailed surveys of representative samples of American college students at five selective US universities, including both public and private schools in the Northeast, the Midwest, and the South, collecting data from over 5,600 students. We found that, during these years, the way students described the political climate on their campus often differed dramatically from what the public saw in headlines and in social media.[1]

Headlines Are Not the Whole Story

News reports have claimed that "Trumpism" divided American campuses. But at the schools we surveyed while Trump was president, opposition to Trumpism actually united liberal and moderate students. The only division we saw is among conservatives. Only about 17% of conservative students at these schools had strongly positive views of Trump, while over 20% had strongly negative views. Even among conservative students, Trump had few supporters at these schools.

News reports during these years also reported that the toxic political climate in Washington, DC, is fracturing campus life along political lines and that conservative students are being ostracized on liberal campuses. Yet liberal and conservative students at most of the campuses we studied were about equally likely to say that they felt like they belonged on campus. At one school we examined, conservative students were actually the most likely to say they felt like they belonged.

Then there's the claim that American campuses are uniformly hostile to the free expression of unpopular ideas, leading students to engage in "self-censorship." But we found a much more complicated story. At Brandeis University and Harvard, more than 60% of liberal students felt that unpopular opinions could not be expressed freely on their campus, and their moderate and conservative peers agreed. Yet, at the

University of Florida, a majority of students, regardless of ideology, felt that their campus was open to the expression of unpopular viewpoints.

The Real Campus Crisis Isn't Politics

Despite these differences, we found that students of a given ideological group tended to have similar views on a variety of hot-button issues regardless of what school they attended, suggesting that national political debates can serve as powerful cues for how students think and talk about politics on any given campus.

It's true too that, during this period, political debates on campus sometimes became so contentious that they dramatically affected campus life. This was the case at Evergreen State College in 2017, where conflicts surrounding a protest against racism on campus led to a campus-wide lockdown.

Other research we've done, though, tells us that for many students the biggest concerns are not politics or discrimination or free expression, or the other issues that dominate headlines about campus conflict.[2] Rather, they are worried about how they will pay their student loans, whether they will pass their next exam, or just how they can stop feeling sad or lonely.

Since we conducted these studies, the situation on college campuses has changed dramatically, especially due to the disruptions of the COVID-19 pandemic and to widespread protests related to the Israel-Hamas war. But even before the pandemic, we already had strong evidence that there was a real mental health crisis on campus.

Unlike most of the claims about political divisions on campus, campus mental health has been the subject of

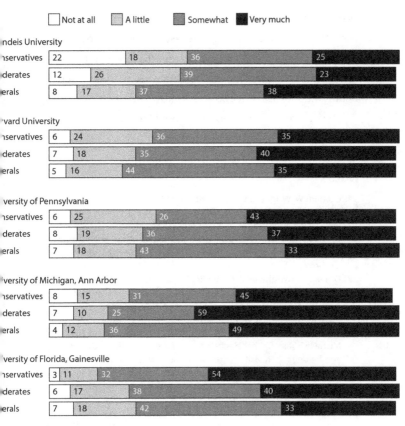

Students at five universities were asked how much they felt like they "belonged" at their school. They responded with "not at all," "a little," "somewhat," or "very much." Their responses are presented as percentages for three subgroups of self-reported political identification: "conservative," "moderate," or "liberal." Percentages may not total 100% in every bar because of rounding.

The Conversation, CC–BY–ND. Data from Brandeis University's Steinhardt Social Research Institute systematic research,[3] and it surfaced in our own studies as well.[4] In 2018 Yale psychology professor Laurie Santos witnessed the scope of the problem firsthand when she offered a new class on happiness. One-quarter of the entire undergraduate student body—over 1,000 students—signed up.

If you want to worry about student life on campus, worry about that.

Notes

1. Graham W. Wright, Shahar Hecht, Michelle Shain, Leonard Saxe, and Stephanie Howland, "Politics on the Quad: Students Report on Division and Disagreement at Five US Universities," Brandeis University, 2019. https://scholarworks.brandeis.edu/esploro/outputs /report/Politics-on-the-Quad-Students-Report/992408824670 1921#file-0.
2. Graham W. Wright, Michelle Shain, Shahar Hecht, and Leonard Saxe, "The Limits of Hostility: Students Report on Antisemitism and Anti-Israel Sentiment at Four US Universities," Brandeis University, 2017. https://scholarworks.brandeis.edu/esploro/outputs/report/The -Limits-of-Hostility/9924088139001921#file-0; Graham W. Wright, Michelle Shain, Shahar Hecht, and Leonard Saxe, "Race, Community, and Belonging: Revisiting Student Concerns at Brandeis University," Brandeis University, 2019. https://scholarworks.brandeis.edu/esploro /outputs/report/Race-Community-and-Belonging-Revisiting -Student/9924088246601921#file-0.
3. Sarah Ketchen Lipson, Emily G. Lattie, and Daniel Eisenberg, "Increased Rates of Mental Health Service Utilization by U.S. College Students: 10-Year Population-Level Trends (2007–2017)," *Psychiatric Services* 70, no. 1 (January 2019): 60–63. https://doi.org/10.1176/appi .ps.201800332.
4. Michelle Shain, Fern Chertok, Graham W. Wright, Shahar Hecht, Richard J Gelles, and Leonard Saxe, "Diversity, Pressure, and Divisions on the University of Pennsylvania Campus," Brandeis University, 2016. https://scholarworks.brandeis.edu/esploro/outputs/report/Diversity -Pressure-and-Divisions-on-the/9924088243701921#file-0.

Chapter 37

Why Colleges Should Think Twice before Punishing Student Protesters

JERUSHA OSBERG CONNER, *Villanova University*

FOR MUCH OF THE 2019–20 ACADEMIC YEAR, Syracuse
University was besieged by student protests over how the
school handled a series of racist incidents on campus. At one
point, Syracuse student activists occupied the campus
administration building. Using the hashtag #NotAgainSU,
they called for action in the wake of racist, anti-Semitic, and
bias-related incidents that allegedly occurred on campus
since they had staged an earlier sit-in to protest a spate of
hate-speech acts on campus. The school initially suspended

30 students involved in the later occupation. Chancellor Kent Syverud lifted the suspensions two days later.

Among other things, the student protestors' demands included hiring more faculty of color and more counselors, revising the curriculum, giving students with disabilities preference in housing, and disarming public safety officers. They also sought to establish new policies for reporting bias-related incidents at the 150-year-old institution, which is located in central New York State and serves more than 15,000 undergraduates.

School officials at Syracuse University acknowledged that they are searching for answers. "We all messed this up and I'm sorry," said Amanda Nicholson, the assistant provost and dean of student success. "What we know is our current policies on how we work with protests have failed. They don't work. This is not a workable situation. We need to come up with something that really does work."[1]

Whereas some may view student protests as something to be squelched, I, an education researcher who studies student activism, have come to see that campus protests, like the ones at Syracuse, serve an important educational purpose.

Student activists have called out their colleges for a variety of things—from relying on overseas sweatshops to produce their college apparel, to polluting the environment, and to doing too little to investigate and punish sexual assault and harassment on campus. Through their activism, students learn not only to recognize and confront what they see as an unjust state of affairs but also to identify the root causes of a problem and develop solutions. The question that college leaders and the broader society must ask, then, is whether punishing student protesters—which is what initially took place at Syracuse—is the right course of action.

Thinking Ahead

I have found that student activists today are quite sophisticated when they seek to negotiate and develop strategies for change.

Consider an example from my 2020 book,[2] in which student activists sought to persuade campus administrators to replace what they saw as a culturally insensitive mascot. They figured that petitions, bookstore boycotts, and other such actions would not get the administration to budge. So they crafted a compromise position to offer, once those other tactics would fail. The compromise would be to require all first-year students to take a course in the history and culture of the people represented by the mascot.

Privately, the student activists reasoned that as more students became educated on why it is problematic for people from a dominant culture to use an oppressed group's identity as a mascot, support for changing the mascot would grow. Publicly, they would present the compromise to administrators as a relatively low-cost and responsible way to address the activists' concerns.

The protesters at Syracuse University pursued similar tactics and goals. For instance, their list of demands included creating a course on the history of protests on their campus.

Learning beyond the Classroom

Research affirms the idea that through activism, students develop critical analysis skills and a deeper understanding of society and social change.[3] Robert Rhoads, a scholar of higher education, found that activism teaches students things they are unlikely to learn from course materials or class discussions.[4] My own research, however, finds that activism can complement academic learning.

For instance, in my study of more than 200 student activists at 120 colleges and universities across the United States, I found that most believed their activism enhanced their academic performance. Although some acknowledged that activist work could feel more important or pressing than a homework assignment, the students by and large credited their activism with making them more successful academically. In some cases, it enabled them to make connections to theory or to apply course material to their everyday life. In other cases, it inspired them to work harder in classes so they would be seen as intellectually credible. Only 12.5% said activism hurt their grades or academic engagement.

Looking to the Future

Sometimes colleges don't recognize the value of student activists until long after the fact. For instance, in 2020, the University of Mississippi—better known as Ole Miss— welcomed back five former students who had been expelled 50 years earlier for protesting a campus environment that was hostile to minority students. The events were intended to honor the sacrifice of the activists and acknowledge the harm they had suffered from law enforcement and university administrators.

I don't think it should take half a century for a university— and society in general—to figure out that punishing students who challenge their institution to improve is a mistake. Fortunately, Syracuse Chancellor Syverud recognized that it was wrong to expel protesters when he reversed the #NotAgainSU suspensions.

The deeper challenge for all universities, in my view, is to figure out how to address the conditions that give rise to protest in the first place.

Notes

1. Quoted in Trish Kilgannon, "#NotAgainSU Protesters Negotiate with SU Administrators," Spectrum News, March 2, 2020. https://spectrumlocalnews.com/nys/central-ny/news/2020/03/03/not-again-su-meets-with-administrators.
2. Jerusha O. Conner, The New Student Activists: The Rise of Neoactivism on College Campuses (Baltimore: Johns Hopkins University Press, 2020).
3. Roderick J. Watts, Matthew A. Diemer, and Adam M. Voight, "Critical Consciousness: Current Status and Future Directions," New Directions for Child and Adolescent Development, no. 134 (December 6, 2011): 43–57. https://doi.org/10.1002/cd.310; Adrianna Kezar, "Faculty and Staff Partnering with Student Activists: Unexplored Terrains of Interaction and Development," Journal of College Student Development 51, no. 5 (2010): 451–80. https://doi.org/10.1353/csd.2010.0001.
4. Robert A. Rhoads, "Student Activism, Diversity, and the Struggle for a Just Society," Journal of Diversity in Higher Education 9, no. 3 (2016): 189–202. https://doi.org/10.1037/dhe0000039.

Contributors

ASIM ALI, PhD, holds a Bachelor's in Software Engineering, a Master's in Information Systems Management, and a Doctorate in Adult Education from Auburn University. As the Executive Director of the Biggio Center at Auburn, Dr. Ali advances professional development programs and resources to enhance instructional innovation and to support scholarly and creative activities. Dr. Ali co-leads work on artificial intelligence to build faculty capacity for understanding and implementing it. Dr. Ali has modeled the implementation of generative AI in the introductory course on information systems he teaches. He has been an invited keynote speaker and presenter at national conferences and many universities.

ISIS ARTZE-VEGA, EdD, serves as the Provost and Vice President for Academic Affairs at Valencia College in Central Florida, a Hispanic-serving institution that serves about 70,000 students annually and has long been regarded as one of the nation's best community colleges. Prior to joining Valencia, Artze-Vega served as the Assistant Vice President for Teaching and Learning at Florida International University, before which she taught English composition and enrollment management at the University of Miami. She is the editor and lead author of the *Norton Guide to Equity-Minded Teaching* and a coauthor of *Connections Are Everything: A College Student's Guide to Relationship-Rich Education*.

ALICIA BENCOMO GARCIA is a member of the Ethnic Studies Faculty and its Department Chair at Cabrillo College. Her research is accountable to minoritized students who experience academic probation or academic disqualification and those who are reinstated. Through her work, she challenges institutions to better serve students, by pulling them in instead of pushing them out, when they encounter academic challenges.

NICHOLAS A. BOWMAN is the Mary Louise Petersen Chair in Higher Education, a Professor of Educational Policy and Leadership Studies, a Senior Research Fellow in the Public Policy Center, and the Director of the Center for Research on Undergraduate Education at the University of Iowa. His research uses a social psychological lens to explore key issues in higher education, including student success, diversity and equity, rankings, admissions, and research methodology. His work has appeared in over 100 journal articles, which include prestigious outlets such as the *Review of Educational Research*, *Educational Researcher*, *Sociology of Education*, *Social Psychological and Personality Science*, *Science Advances*, and *Science*.

ALEXA CAPELOTO is an Associate Professor at John Jay College of Criminal Justice, City University of New York, where she teaches journalism and co-coordinates the college's Digital Media and Journalism Minor. She also is the Faculty Adviser for the college's student news publication, the *John Jay Sentinel*. She earned her master's degree from Columbia University's Graduate School of Journalism in 2000 and worked as a Reporter and Editor at the *Detroit Free Press* and the *San Diego Union-Tribune*. Since joining the John Jay faculty in 2009, she has published several legal, scholarly, and journalistic articles related to freedom of information laws, paying particular attention to the intersection of privatization and the public's right to know.

CELESTE K. CARRUTHERS is the Fox Distinguished Professor of Labor Economics in the Haslam College of Business at the University of Tennessee with a joint appointment in the Department of Economics and the Boyd Center for Business and Economic Research. Her research centers on education policy with crossovers into public economics, labor economics, and economic history. Recent and ongoing projects examine financial aid, college choices, career and technical education, and the consequences of segregated schools in the United States in the early twentieth century. She teaches graduate and undergraduate courses in public economics and econometrics. Carruthers is the Editor-in-Chief of *Economics of Education Review*.

MONNICA CHAN is an Assistant Professor at the University of Massachusetts, Boston. Her research explores the effect of higher education policies on student access and success, particularly in the areas of college affordability and public financing of higher education institutions.

MARY L. CHURCHILL is a Professor of the Practice and the Associate Dean of Strategic Partnerships and Community Engagement at Boston University's Wheelock College of Education and Human Development, where she also serves as the Director of the Higher Education Administration Program. Churchill serves as a trustee at Benjamin Franklin Cummings Institute of Technology, a four-year minority-serving college in Boston, where she chairs the academic affairs committee. She also serves as an advisor for the American Council of Education's Learner Success Lab. Churchill coauthored *When Colleges Close: Leading in a Time of Crisis*, telling the story of the Wheelock–Boston University merger.

DEBORAH COHN is a Provost Professor of Spanish and Portuguese at Indiana University Bloomington. She is the author of *The Latin American Literary Boom and U.S. Nationalism during the Cold War* (Vanderbilt University Press) and *History and Memory in the Two Souths: Recent Southern and Spanish American Fiction* (Vanderbilt University Press) as well as the coeditor of *International Education at the Crossroads* (Indiana University Press) and *Look Away! The U.S. South in New World Studies* (Duke University Press). She has received fellowships from the National Endowment for the Humanities, the Rockefeller Archive Center, the American Philosophical Society, and the Harry Ransom Center, among other sources.

MAX COLEMAN is an Assistant Professor of Sociology at the University of Utah. His research centers on the psychological consequences of social stratification, with a particular focus on common mental health conditions such as major depression. His teaching interests include medical sociology and social psychology.

FELECIA COMMODORE is an Associate Professor of Higher Education in the College of Education at the University of Illinois, Urbana-Champaign. Her research concerns leadership, governance, and administrative practices, with a particular focus on historically Black colleges and universities and minority-serving institutions. She also researches organizational culture and behavior; the role of boards in achieving educational equity; how leadership is exercised, constructed, and viewed in various communities; and the relationship between Black women and leadership. She is the lead author of *Black Women College Students: A Guide to Success in Higher Education*. She earned her PhD in Higher Education from the University of Pennsylvania's Graduate School of Education.

JERUSHA OSBERG CONNER is a Professor of Education at Villanova University. She has expertise in student voice, student engagement, and youth organizing and activism. The author of more than 65 peer-reviewed journal articles and book chapters, she wrote *The New Student Activists* (Johns Hopkins University Press) and coedited *The Handbook on Youth Activism* (Edward Elgar), *The International Handbook of Student Voice in Higher Education* (Bloomsbury), and *Contemporary Youth Activism* (ABC-CLIO).

MARCELA G. CUELLAR is an Associate Professor in the School of Education at the University of California, Davis. Her research examines higher education access and equity with a focus on Latinx/a/o student experiences and outcomes at Hispanic-serving institutions, campus climate, and community college baccalaureates. Her scholarship has been published in the *American Journal of Education*, *Community College Review*, *Journal of Higher Education*, *Review of Higher Education*, and *Teachers College Record*.

DAWN KIYOE CULPEPPER (she/her) is the Director of the University of Maryland's ADVANCE Program for Inclusive Excellence. Dr. Culpepper's research examines diversity, equity, and inclusion in the academic workplace. She focuses on policies, practices, and resources that foster equity, disrupt bias, spur organizational effectiveness, and create conditions where faculty thrive. She has held leadership roles on several projects funded by the National Science Foundation. Dr. Culpepper leverages research to inform practice, leading faculty development and educational initiatives across UMD's campus. She completed her BA in Government at the University of Virginia, her MEd in Higher Education Administration at North Carolina State University, and her PhD in Higher Education at the University of Maryland.

WALTER G. ECTON is an Assistant Professor in the University of Michigan's Center for the Study of Higher and Postsecondary Education. His research lies at the intersections among high school, higher education, the workforce, and the pathways students take in navigating those sectors. His work primarily focuses on students who take nontraditional pathways through education, with particular focuses on high school students in career and technical education, students who attend college, and students who return to education later in life.

PETER FELTEN is the Executive Director of the Center for Engaged Learning, a Professor of History, and the Assistant Provost for Teaching and Learning at Elon University. He has had published seven books about undergraduate education, including *Connections Are Everything: A College Student's Guide to Relationship-Rich Education* (Johns Hopkins University Press, 2023), coauthored with Isis Artze-Vega, Leo M. Lambert, and Oscar R. Miranda Tapia and available in an open-access online edition free to all readers. He serves on the advisory board of the National Survey of Student Engagement and is a Fellow of the Gardner Institute.

LAUREN FOLEY is an Assistant Professor in the Department of Political Science and the Director of the Capital Internship Program at Western Michigan University. Dr. Foley is the author of *On the Basis of Race: How Higher Education Navigates Affirmative Action Policies* (New York University Press, 2023). Her work has also appeared in the *Journal of Political Science Education; Studies in Law, Politics, and Society*; and the *Journal of Law and Education*. She was admitted to the Michigan Bar Association in 2009.

MNEESHA GELLMAN is an Associate Professor of Political Science in the Marlboro Institute for Liberal Arts and Interdisciplinary Studies at Emerson College. Her research spans human rights, democratization, and education politics across the globe. Dr. Gellman serves as an expert witness on El Salvador and Mexico in asylum proceedings in US immigration courts and is the Founder and Director of the Emerson Prison Initiative, which brings a bachelor's degree pathway to people incarcerated in Massachusetts.

ERIC GRODSKY is a Professor of Sociology and Educational Policy at the University of Wisconsin, Madison. He does research on education across the life course—from four-year-old kindergarten through the ways in which educational opportunities and experiences shape health outcomes later in life. With Chandra Muller and Rob Warren, he is a co–principal investigator on the EdSHARe projects called High School and Beyond and the National Longitudinal Study of the Class of 1972. With Beth Vaade and Katie Eklund, he codirects the Madison Education Partnership, a research-practice partnership between the Wisconsin Center for Education Research and the Madison Metropolitan School District.

CAROLYN J. HEINRICH is the Patricia and Rodes Hart Professor of Public Policy, Education and Economics in the Peabody College of

Education and Human Development at Vanderbilt University and is a University Distinguished Professor of Leadership, Policy, and Organizations in Peabody College and of Political Science in the College of Arts and Science. She also holds secondary appointments as a Professor of Health Policy in the Vanderbilt University School of Medicine and a Professor of Economics in the Department of Economics, College of Arts and Science.

AUDREY J. JAEGER, PhD, is the W. Dallas Herring Professor of Community College Education at North Carolina State University's College of Education and the founding Executive Director of the Belk Center for Community College Leadership and Research. Jaeger's commitment to the accessibility and attainment of high-quality postsecondary education for each and every student is a natural expansion of her decades of research that explores community colleges, leadership, faculty development, college transfer, and gender issues in higher education. Contributing to the growing body of research about student outcomes and institutional effectiveness, her work advances student success by bringing actionable data to leaders and policy makers in North Carolina and beyond.

GEORGE JUSTICE is the Provost and a Professor of English at the University of Tulsa. From 2013 to 2017, he served as the Dean of Humanities and Associate Vice President for Arts and Humanities at Arizona State University. A specialist in eighteenth-century British literature, Justice is an author and editor of scholarship on the literary marketplace, authorship, and women's writing. Justice previously taught at the University of Pennsylvania, Marquette University, Louisiana State University, and the University of Missouri, where he also served as the Vice Provost for Advanced Studies and the Dean of the Graduate School. His book *How to Be a Dean* was published in 2019 by Johns Hopkins University Press.

ARIELLE KUPERBERG is an Associate Professor of Sociology at the University of Maryland, Baltimore County, and the Chair of the Council on Contemporary Families. She has authored over 20 peer-reviewed articles on topics related to families, relationships, and young adulthood with student loans.

ALEXANDRA KUVAEVA is a Postdoctoral Associate at the University of Maryland. As a Graduate Research Assistant pursuing a doctorate degree, she worked for the ADVANCE Program for Inclusive Excellence at the University of Maryland, College Park, a campus-wide project supported by the National Science Foundation that promotes institutional transformation in the retention and advancement of women faculty in STEM disciplines by contributing to quantitative and qualitative data collection and analysis. Her graduate work consolidated her deep interest in higher education policies and practices and shaped her career trajectory as a researcher focusing on issues affecting faculty careers.

LEO M. LAMBERT is a Professor of Education and President Emeritus of Elon University, where he served as president from 1999 to 2018. During his tenure as president, Lambert led two 10-year strategic plans for the campus that propelled Elon from a regional college to a university of national distinction. A chapter of Phi Beta Kappa, the oldest and most prestigious academic honor society in the United States, was established at Elon in 2010 following major investments in the liberal arts and sciences, experiential learning programs, the honors program, and faculty development. Elon's professional schools of business, law, health sciences, communications, and education achieved top accreditations and distinctions during his presidency.

RAYNA M. LETOURNEAU, PhD, RN, is the Executive Director of the Florida Center for Nursing and an Associate Professor in the University of South Florida's College of Nursing. She has more than 20 years of nursing experience. She earned her Bachelor of Science in Nursing and Master of Science in Nursing Administration from the University of Rhode Island and her PhD in Nursing from the University of Massachusetts, Dartmouth. Dr. Letourneau's scholarship focuses on nursing workforce development. She has numerous publications and presentations. In 2022 Dr. Letourneau was named to the Florida Health Care Power 100 by City & State Florida.

ERICA JACQUELINE LICHT has been engaged in racial equity and organizational change research and training for over 15 years. Most recently she served as the Research Projects Director at the Institutional Antiracism and Accountability Project (IARA) at Harvard University, where she led and co-designed IARA's projects and partnerships. Licht is a Fulbright Scholar and holds a Master's in Public Administration from the Harvard Kennedy School and a Master's in Justice Policy from the London School of Economics, where she was a Maguire Fellow. She is a Lecturer at the Harvard Extension School on the topic of equitable institutional change, and her writing has appeared in the *New York Times*, *Boston Globe*, and CNN. She cohosts the podcast *Untying Knots*.

SUZANNA M. MARTINEZ, MS, PhD, is an Associate Professor at the University of California, San Francisco, in the Department of Epidemiology and Biostatistics. She researches food insecurity's impact across the life course as well as the interconnectedness of diet, physical activity, sleep, and weight in preventing cardiometabolic diseases.

JOAN MAYA MAZELIS is an Associate Professor of Sociology in the Department of Sociology, Anthropology & Criminal Justice and the Director of the Gender Studies Program at Rutgers University–Camden. She is also a Faculty Affiliate at the University of Wisconsin's Institute for Research on Poverty and a member of the Council on Contemporary Families and of the Scholars Strategy Network. Dr. Mazelis is the author of *Surviving Poverty: Creating Sustainable Ties among the Poor* (New York University Press, 2017).

MARK MCNEILLY, a Professor of Business at the University of North Carolina, Chapel Hill, specializes in marketing and organizational behavior. He previously worked as a global marketing executive in the information technology industry for IBM and Lenovo. McNeilly authored three books, including *Sun Tzu and the Art of Business*. He has shared his expertise on strategy and marketing globally, with appearances on the BBC, C-SPAN, and CNBC, and was featured in a History Channel special on Sun Tzu's *Art of War*. McNeilly also contributes as an expert blogger for *Fast Company* magazine.

OSCAR R. MIRANDA TAPIA is a Research Associate at the Belk Center for Community College Leadership and Research and a Graduate Research Assistant at the William and Ida Friday Institute for Educational Innovation at North Carolina State University, where he is a Provost Fellow pursuing a PhD in Educational Leadership, Policy, and Human Development with a concentration on higher education opportunity, equity, and justice. Before pursuing his degree, he led the first-generation initiative at Elon University. He is a coauthor of *Connections Are Everything: A College Student's Guide to Relationship-Rich Education* and holds degrees from Elon University and Harvard University.

JOYA MISRA is a Distinguished Professor of Sociology and Public Policy at the University of Massachusetts, Amherst. Her work has appeared in the *American Sociological Review, American Journal of Sociology, Gender & Society, Social Forces, Social Problems*, and numerous other professional journals and edited volumes. She edited the journal *Gender & Society*, a top-ranked journal in both gender studies and sociology, from 2011 to 2015, and was the 2023–24 President of the American Sociological Association.

JOHANN N. NEEM is a Professor of American History at Western Washington University. His scholarship has concerned the political and intellectual history of the early American republic. He has also written extensively about contemporary reform in K–12 and higher education. He is the author of three books: *What's the Point of College? Seeking Purpose in an Age of Reform* (2019), *Democracy's Schools: The Rise* *of Public Education in America* (2017), and *Creating a Nation of Joiners: Democracy and Civil Society in Early National Massachusetts* (2008).

DAVID J. NGUYEN is an Associate Professor of Higher Education and Student Affairs at Ohio University. He holds a BS in Accounting and Marketing Management and an MS in Accounting, both from Syracuse University. He also holds an MS in College Student Development and Counseling from Northeastern University and a PhD in Higher, Adult & Lifelong Education from Michigan State University. Dr. Nguyen's teaching and research interests focus on access and equity issues in postsecondary education.

KERRYANN O'MEARA is the Vice President for Academic Affairs, Provost, and a Professor in the Higher and Postsecondary Education Program in the Organization and Leadership Department of Teachers College, Columbia University. Her scholarship and leadership are highly integrated and focus on creating a more diverse and inclusive academic workplace. She has designed, tested, and shared evidence-based strategies to remove barriers and improve full participation for scholars from historically minoritized groups, with particular attention paid to faculty hiring, retention, workload, and evaluation.

MOLLY OTT is an Associate Professor of Higher and Postsecondary Education at Arizona State University. Her research considers organizational issues in higher education, especially how colleges and universities can improve faculty and staff experiences in the workplace and support their career success. Among other outlets, her scholarship has been published in *Research in Higher Education*, *Review of Higher Education*, and the *Journal of Higher Education*. She is an Associate Editor for *Educational Policy Analysis Archives* and serves on the editorial board of the *Journal of Education Human Resources*.

TIMOTHY POYNTON is a Professor and Counselor Educator committed to improving the transition from high school into young adulthood through his research and teaching. A former School Counselor, Dr. Poynton is currently an Associate Professor in the Department of Counseling & School Psychology at the University of Massachusetts, Boston. Dr. Poynton has published several research articles, book chapters, and a book related to school counseling, career development, and college readiness. He was recognized in 2011 as the Counselor Educator of the Year by the American School Counselor Association.

JAYMES PYNE studies the nature and consequences of engagement, punishment, and inequality in social institutions. He earned his PhD from the University of Wisconsin, Madison's Department of Sociology in August 2019. Currently he is a Senior Research Associate at Stanford's Graduate School of Education.

TIMOTHY J. RYAN is a Professor of Political Science at the University of North Carolina, Chapel Hill. He focuses on public opinion, political psychology, and political behavior.

KEM SAICHAIE (he/him) is the Executive Director of the Center for Educational Effectiveness at the University of California, Davis. He works with faculty and graduate students across disciplines to investigate and integrate evidence-based and equity-focused pedagogical practices in face-to-face, hybrid, and online learning spaces. He has published in a number of venues including the *Journal of Higher Education, PLOS One, International Journal for the Scholarship of Teaching and Learning, New Directions in Teaching and Learning,* and *Encyclopedia of International Higher Education Systems and Institutions.*

MICHELLE SAMURA is the Dean of Arts, Humanities, and Social Sciences at Santiago Canyon College. Her research interests center on the relationship among space, belonging, and community. As an interdisciplinary scholar, Samura draws upon insights from design, architecture, critical geography, education, and sociology to identify key design principles and elements of built environments that promote belonging in education, the workplace, health care, hospitality, and community settings.

LEONARD SAXE is the Klutznick Professor of Contemporary Jewish Studies and the Director of the Cohen Center for Modern Jewish Studies and the Steinhardt Social Research Institute at Brandeis University. He is a former Congressional Science Fellow and the recipient of awards from the American Psychological Association and the Association for the Scientific Study of Jewry. Saxe is a social psychologist concerned with the application of social science to social policy issues. His present focus is on religious and ethnic identity and specifically addresses issues related to Judaism and engagement with the Jewish community and Israel.

MICHAEL SIMKOVIC is the Leon Benwell Professor of Law and Accounting at the University of Southern California's Gould School of Law.

KATIE N. SMITH is an Associate Professor of Higher Education at Temple University. Smith's research focuses on equity issues as they relate to college students' career development experiences and postgraduate outcomes.

STEPHANIE SOWL, PhD, is a Program Officer at ECMC Foundation, leading its Rural Impact Initiative. Her research explores the relationship between spatial inequality and postsecondary opportunities, particularly as it relates to rural, first-generation, and/or working-class students. She also is interested in adults' residential mobility patterns over time, specifically trends associated with different educational levels, postsecondary institutional types, and community contexts.

NICHOLAS TAMPIO is a Professor of Political Science at Fordham University. Tampio researches the history of political thought, contemporary political theory, and education policy. He is the editor of John Dewey's *Democracy and Education* (Columbia University Press, 2024) and author of *Teaching Political Theory: A Pluralistic Approach* (Edward Elgar Publishing, 2022).

SHITAL THEKDI is an Associate Professor of Analytics and Operations in the Robins School of Business at the University of Richmond. She earned a PhD in Systems and Information Engineering at the University of Virginia and an MSE and BSE in Industrial and Operations Engineering at the University of Michigan. She teaches courses in analytics and decision-making. Her research focuses on risk analysis and management in operations.

ELENA G. VAN STEE is a PhD Candidate in Sociology at the University of Pennsylvania and an Exchange Scholar at Harvard University. Van Stee edits the blog for *Contexts*, the public-facing magazine of the American Sociological Association. She studies culture and inequality, focusing on social class, families, higher education, and the transition to adulthood.

BRADFORD VIVIAN (PhD, Pennsylvania State University) is a Professor of Rhetoric in the Department of Communication Arts and Sciences at Penn State. His most recent book is *Campus Misinformation: The Real Threat to Free Speech in American Higher Education* (Oxford University Press). Vivian's other books include *Commonplace Witnessing: Rhetorical Invention, Historical Remembrance, and Public Culture* (Oxford University Press) and *Public Forgetting: The Rhetoric and Politics of Beginning Again* (Penn State Press). He is a recipient of the James A. Winans–Herbert A. Wichelns Award for Distinguished Scholarship in Rhetoric and Public Address and the Penn State Class of 1933: Distinction in the Humanities Award.

WALTER V. WENDLER became President of West Texas A&M University in 2016. He previously served as the Chancellor of Southern Illinois University, Carbondale, from 2001 to 2007, before returning to teaching architecture. He is a distinguished alumnus of the College of

Architecture at Texas A&M University, where he served for 18 years in numerous administrative roles, including Dean and Executive Assistant to the President. He also served for two years as Vice Chancellor of the Texas A&M University System. Wendler is a vocal university leader who has written weekly op-eds for nearly two decades on topics related to higher education.

GERALD WHITTINGTON is Senior Vice President Emeritus at Elon University. He was also the Vice President for Business and Finance at Agnes Scott College and served in the administration at the University of Virginia, Duke University, and the University of North Carolina, Chapel Hill. Whittington was named the 2018 Distinguished Business Officer by the National Association of College and University Business Officers, its highest award and honor. He has an undergraduate degree from the University of North Carolina, Chapel Hill, and an MSM/MBA from Duke University. Whittington is regularly a national speaker on the topic of higher education finance.

CLAIRE WLADIS is a Professor of Mathematics at the Borough of Manhattan Community College of the City University of New York (CUNY) and of Urban Education at the CUNY Graduate Center. She currently leads the Equity through Education Research Group at CUNY and is the lead principal investigator on three research projects funded by grants from the National Science Foundation: one focused on creating and validating the Algebra Concept Inventory; one on assessing the extent to which the availability of online courses provides better access to STEM degrees; and one on exploring which factors impact the trajectories of mathematics majors at community colleges.

GRAHAM WRIGHT is an Associate Research Scientist at the Steinhardt Social Research Institute and an Associate Research Professor in the Heller School for Social Policy and Management at Brandeis University. His research exploring the intersection of American political attitudes and identities has been published in the journals *Political Behavior*; *Politics and Religion*; *Politics, Groups, and Identities*; and *Sociological Inquiry*. His work on deliberative democracy has been published in the *Journal of Deliberative Democracy* and in a forthcoming book from Routledge. His current work explores the interplay of antisemitism and politics on the college campus.

PATRICIA A. YOUNG is the Chairperson and a Professor of the Department of Education at the University of Maryland, Baltimore County. She is the 2023 recipient of the Indiana University School of Education Dean's Medallion, a lifetime achievement award for individuals who have contributed to the betterment of society through education. Dr. Young developed the culture-based model as a framework for building culture-based information and communication technologies. Her book *Human Specialization in Design and Technology: The Current Wave for Learning, Culture, Industry, and Beyond* (2021) advocates for innovation as the way to improve industry, education, and human performance.

THOMAS ZIMMERMAN is a doctoral candidate in the PhD in Higher Education Program at Rutgers University. He researches state funding for higher education, higher education law, and student outcomes. His background includes over a decade of professional experience in various positions in higher education, and he currently serves as a Research and Data Associate in New Jersey's Office of the Secretary of Higher Education.

Index

ethics and AI, 185
eugenics, 11–12

faculty: and AI, 172, 186–88; burnout, 172, 179; compensation, 194; declines in, 186–90; diversity of, 138, 146–49, 152; diversity work by, 138, 152, 161–64, 168; mental health of, 172, 179; and mental health of students, 175–79; non–tenure track, 173, 189, 201; office hours, 35; relationships in mentoring students, 3, 34–36; satisfaction, 152; self-care, 172, 179; shortages in, 172–73, 191–94; and workload equity, 164. *See also* academic freedom; mentors; tenure
Faculty Workload and Rewards Project, 162–64
FAFSA (Free Application for Federal Student Aid), 22–23
FAFSA Simplification Act, 23
FairTest, 13
financial aid: advisers, 24; applying for, 22–23; and childcare, 124; and earnings potential, 67–71; and financial responsibility composite score, 100; and food insecurity, 129; and for-profit institutions, 103, 106, 107; and GPA, 7; and private schools, 95–96; strategies for, 22–23, 24; and working students, xxx, 47. *See also* loans, student
financial responsibility composite score, 100
first-generation students: and direct admissions, xxiv; diversity and performance of, 151; and giving back, 63–66; and loans, 31; and relationships, 34–38; school selection tips, 5–9; working, 47
flipped classrooms, 189–90
food insecurity and hunger, xxvii, 110, 126–30
forbearance, for loans, 23, 25
foreign-language enrollment, 73–78
for-profit institutions, 82, 102–7
foundations, charitable, 61, 67–71, 85–90
4+1 programs, xxix
Free Application for Federal Student Aid (FAFSA), 22–23

friends, 3, 34–38. *See also* peers
funding: declines in, 59, 113; means-tested, 95; secrecy of private foundations, 85–90; for tuition-free programs, 94

gainful employment regulations, 106
García, Mildred, 68
Gates Foundation, 61, 67–71
gender: and enrollments, xv; and tenure, 201; and time poverty, 122–23. *See also* women
George Mason University, 85–88
Gooblar, David, 178
GPA (grade point average), xxiii, 7, 11, 17, 123, 127, 144
graduate school programs, xvii, xxix, 40–43, 129
graduation rates / degree completion: and diversity of faculty, 146–49; and diversity programs, 151; percentage of Americans with degrees, 131; and race, 59, 138, 146–49; and school resources, 93; and selecting schools, 6–7; student-parents, 123; working students, 3, 45–48
grants: defined, 24; and earnings potential, 67, 70; nursing programs, 194; Pell Grants, 22, 30, 47, 129, 131–35; prison education programs, 131–35
Guttman, Amy, 166

health benefits of higher education, xix, xxx, 50, 82, 113
health care: costs, xxvii, 110, 111–14; shortages in, 172–73, 191–94
higher education: current state of, xiv–xvii; decline in demand for, xiii–xiv, xix–xxi; decline in number of graduates, 59; decline in perception of value, ix–x; global rankings, xvi–xvii, 59; number of institutions, 5. *See also* admissions; enrollments; faculty; students; tuition
Higher Education Act, 68, 70
high schools. *See* secondary schools
holistic admissions, 143
Hopwood v. Texas, 142
housing, xxvii, xxx, 110, 116–18, 222
Human Development Index (HDI), xvi
hunger. *See* food insecurity and hunger

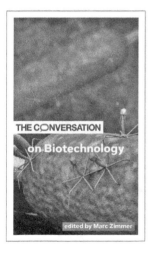